Mercury Reader for English 103, 3rd edition
Dr. Deanna Davis

ISBN 10: 1-323-35087-X
ISBN 13: 978-1-323-35087-4

General Editors

Janice Neuleib
Illinois State University

Kathleen Shine Cain
Merrimack College

Stephen Ruffus
Salt Lake Community College

Table of Contents

The Triumph of the Yell

Deborah Tannen

Deborah Tannen (1945–), born in Brooklyn, New York, received her Ph.D. in linguistics from the University of California, Berkeley and teaches at Georgetown University. Her research into how people communicate has brought her critical and popular acclaim, and she has appeared on several television programs and has written for The New York Times, The Washington Post, *and* Vogue. *Her book* That's Not what I Meant *(1987) analyzes the effects of conversational styles on relationships.* You Just Don't Understand *(1990) examines differences in how men and women converse.* Talking From 9 to 5 *(1994) resulted from her research into conversational styles in work settings and their impact on how work is performed and who gets ahead. The following essay, which first appeared in* The New York Times *in 1994, discusses what happens when public discourse takes on the characteristics of having an argument. As you read it, think about current issues in the press and how some journalists turn complex issues into a simple battle of sound bytes between two sides.*

1   I put the question to a journalist who had written a vitriolic attack   1
on a leading feminist researcher: "Why do you need to make others wrong for you to be right?" Her response: "It's an argument!"
   That's the problem. More and more these days, journalists, politicians and academics treat public discourse as an argument—not in the sense of *making* an argument, but in the sense of *having* one, of having a fight.

When people have arguments in private life, they're not trying to understand what the other person is saying. They're listening for weaknesses in logic to leap on, points they can distort to make the other look bad. We all do this when we're angry, but is it the best model for public intellectual interchange? This breakdown of the boundary between public and private is contributing to what I have come to think of as a culture of critique.

Fights have winners and losers. If you're fighting to win, the temptation is great to deny facts that support your opponent's views and present only those facts that support your own.

5   At worst, there's a temptation to lie. We accept this style of arguing because we believe we can tell when someone is lying. But we can't. Paul Ekman, a psychologist at the University of California at San Francisco, has found that even when people are very sure they can tell whether or not someone is dissembling, their judgments are as likely as not to be wrong.

If public discourse is a fight, every issue must have two sides—no more, no less. And it's crucial to show "the other side," even if one has to scour the margins of science or the fringes of lunacy to find it.

The culture of critique is based on the belief that opposition leads to truth: when both sides argue, the truth will emerge. And because people are presumed to enjoy watching a fight, the most extreme views are presented, since they make the best show. But it is a myth that opposition leads to truth when truth does not reside on one side or the other but is rather a crystal of many sides. Truth is more likely to be found in the complex middle than in the simplified extremes, but the spectacles that result when extremes clash are thought to get higher ratings or larger readership.

Because the culture of critique encourages people to attack and often misrepresent others, those others must waste their creativity and time correcting the misrepresentations and defending themselves. Serious scholars have had to spend years of their lives writing books proving that the Holocaust happened, because a few fanatics who claim it didn't have been given a public forum. Those who provide the platform know that what these people say is, simply put, not true, but rationalize the dissemination of lies as showing "the other side." The determination to find another side can spread disinformation rather than lead to truth.

The culture of critique has given rise to the journalistic practice of confronting prominent people with criticism couched as others' views. Meanwhile, the interviewer has planted an accusation in readers' or viewers' minds. The theory seems to be that when provoked, people are spurred to eloquence and self-revelation. Perhaps some are. But others are unable to say what they know because they are hurt, and begin to sputter when their sense of fairness is outraged. In those cases, opposition is not the path to truth.

10   When people in power know that what they say will be scrutinized for weaknesses and probably distorted, they become more guarded. As an acquaintance recently explained about himself, public figures who once gave long, free-wheeling press conferences now limit themselves to reading brief statements. When less information gets communicated, opposition does not lead to truth.

Opposition also limits information when only those who are adept at verbal sparring take part in public discourse, and those who cannot handle it, or do not like it, decline to participate. This winnowing process is evident in graduate schools, where many talented students drop out because what they expected to be a community of intellectual inquiry turned out to be a ritual game of attack and counterattack.

One such casualty graduated from a small liberal arts college, where she "luxuriated in the endless discussions." At the urging of her professors, she decided to make academia her profession. But she changed her mind after a year in an art history program at a major university. She felt she had fallen into a "den of wolves." "I wasn't cut out for academia," she concluded. But does academia have to be so combative that it cuts people like her out?

In many university classrooms, "critical thinking" means reading someone's life work, then ripping it to shreds. Though critique is surely one form of critical thinking, so are integrating ideas from disparate fields and examining the context out of which they grew. Opposition does not lead to truth when we ask only "What's wrong with this argument?" and never "What can we use from this in building a new theory, and a new understanding?"

Several years ago I was on a television talk show with a representative of the men's movement. I didn't foresee any problem, since there is nothing in my work that is anti-male. But in the room where guests gather before the show I found a man wearing a shirt and tie and a floor-length skirt, with waist-length red hair. He politely introduced himself and told me he liked my book. Then he added: "When I get out there, I'm going to attack you. But don't take it personally. That's why they invite me on, so that's what I'm going to do."

15   When the show began, I spoke only a sentence or two before this man nearly jumped out of his chair, threw his arms before him in gestures of anger and began shrieking—first attacking me, but soon moving on to rail against women. The most disturbing thing about his hysterical ranting was what it sparked in the studio audience: they too became vicious, attacking not me (I hadn't had a chance to say anything) and not him (who wants to tangle with someone who will scream at you?) but the other guests: unsuspecting women who had agreed to come on the show to talk about their problems communicating with their spouses.

This is the most dangerous aspect of modeling intellectual interchange as a fight: it contributes to an atmosphere of animosity that spreads like a fever. In a society where people express their anger by shooting, the result of demonizing those with whom we disagree can be truly demonic.

I am not suggesting that journalists stop asking tough questions necessary to get at the facts, even if those questions may appear challenging. And of course it is the responsibility of the media to represent serious opposition when it exists, and of intellectuals everywhere to explore potential weaknesses in others' arguments. But when opposition becomes the overwhelming avenue of inquiry, when the lust for opposition exalts extreme views and obscures complexity, when our eagerness to find weaknesses blinds us to strengths, when the atmosphere of animosity precludes respect and poisons our relations with one another, then the culture of critique is stifling us. If we could move beyond it, we would move closer to the truth.

Questions on Meaning

1. Summarize the problem of public discourse that Tannen describes as "the culture of critique."
2. What does Tannen argue that journalists or others should do about this problem?
3. What happens to the openness of public discourse once it declines into "yelling" and a win-or-lose atmosphere? What are the effects on public figures involved in the debate?

Questions on Rhetorical Strategy and Style

1. Reread Tannen's extended example of the talk show incident where she and other women are verbally attacked. How does this example help develop the ideas she has been developing in that section of the essay?
2. What do you think is Tannen's greater goal in the essay: to demonstrate that the problem exists and explain its effects, or to persuade us what we need to do to go beyond it? What is your evidence for your answer? How does this goal affect her choice of strategies for the writing of the essay?

Writing Assignments

1. Choose two editorials from the Sunday edition of a major metropolitan newspaper. Read and analyze each of them carefully in relation to the following questions. Does the writer assume there are only two positions on the issue being discussed? Is the writer argumentative in the sense of attacking the other position (or a person who represents it) rather than arguing calmly with facts and reason? Does the writer make emotional appeals or even use name calling? Does the writer selectively ignore some facts and perhaps distort others rather than fairly analyzing facts on both sides of the debate? What conclusions overall do you reach about the strength of their arguments?
2. Choose a controversial current social issue that is generally argued on one side or the other. Analyze the elements of these arguments. Are there only two positions possible? Is it a clear-cut choice between two opposing sides? Or is there some middle ground possible, or a third position? Write an essay in which you describe the issue and the possible positions, but do not *argue for* a position. Help your reader see the complexity involved in the issue rather than a simple black-or-white choice.

Abortion Is Too Complex to Feel All One Way About

Anna Quindlen

Anna Quindlen (1953–) grew up in Philadelphia and graduated from Barnard College. She first worked as a journalist for the New York Post *and* The New York Times, *where she became a personal opinion columnist. Her writing for the* Times' *"Hers" column covers many topics such as motherhood, family relations, and marriage, and she wrote her own column called "Life in the Thirties." The best of her columns have been collected in* Living Out Loud *(1988),* Thinking Out Loud *(1993), and* Loud and Clear *(2004). She won the Pulitzer Prize for Commentary in 1992. Her work in fiction includes the novels* Object Lessons *(1997),* One True Thing *(1994),* Black and Blue *(1998), and* Blessings *(2003). The following essay was written as a column for the* Times. *Like many of her columns, it explores a social issue from a personal position.*

1   It was always the look on their faces that told me first. I was the freshman dormitory counselor and they were the freshmen at a women's college where everyone was smart. One of them could come into my room, a golden girl, a valedictorian, an 800 verbal score on the SAT'S, and her eyes would be empty, seeing only a busted future, the devastation of her life as she knew it. She had failed biology, messed up the math; she was pregnant.

That was when I became pro-choice.

It was the look in his eyes that I will always remember, too. They were as black as the bottom of a well, and in them for a few minutes I thought I saw myself the way I had always wished to be—clear, simple, elemental, at peace. My child looked at me and I looked back at him in the delivery room, and I realized that out of a sea of infinite possibilities it had come down to this: a specific person born on the hottest day of the year, conceived on a Christmas Eve, made by his father and me miraculously from scratch.

Once I believed that there was a little blob of formless protoplasm in there and a gynecologist went after it with a surgical instrument, and that was that. Then I got pregnant myself—eagerly, intentionally, by the right man, at the right time—and I began to doubt. My abdomen still flat, my stomach roiling with morning sickness, I felt not that I had protoplasm inside but instead a complete human being in miniature to whom I could talk, sing, make promises. Neither of these views was accurate; instead, I think, the reality is something in the middle, And there is where I find myself now, in the middle, hating the idea of abortions, hating the idea of having them outlawed.

5   For I know it is the right thing in some times and places. I remember sitting in a shabby clinic far uptown with one of those freshman, only three months after the Supreme Court had made what we were doing possible, and watching with wonder as the lovely first love she had had with a nice boy unraveled over the space of an hour as they waited for her to be called, degenerated into sniping and silences. I remember a year or two later seeing them pass on campus and not even acknowledge one another because their conjoining had caused them so much pain, and I shuddered to think of them married, with a small psyche in their unready and unwilling hands.

I've met 14-year-olds who were pregnant and said they could not have abortions because of their religion, and I see in their eyes the shadows of 22-year-olds I've talked to who lost their kids to foster care because they hit them or used drugs or simply had no money for food and shelter. I read not long ago about a teenager who said she meant to have an abortion but she spent the money on clothes instead; now she has a baby who turns out to be a lot more trouble than a toy. The people who hand out those execrable little pictures of dismembered fetuses at abortion clinics seem to forget the extraordinary pain children may endure after they are born when they are unwanted, even hated or simply tolerated.

I believe that in a contest between the living and the almost living, the latter must, if necessary, give way to the will of the former. That is what the fetus is to me, the almost living. Yet these questions began to plague me—and, I've discovered, a good many other women—after I became pregnant. But they became even more acute after I had my second child, mainly because he is so different from his brother. On two random nights 18 months apart the same two people managed to conceive, and on one occasion the tumult within turned itself into a curly-haired brunet with merry black eyes who walked and talked late and loved the whole world, and on another it became a blond with hazel Asian eyes and a pug nose who tried to conquer the world almost as soon as he entered it.

If we were to have an abortion next time for some reason or another, which infinite possibility becomes, not a reality, but a nullity? The girl with the blue eyes? The improbable redhead? The natural athlete? The thinker? My husband, ever at the heart of the matter, put it another way. Knowing that he is finding two children somewhat more overwhelming than he expected, I asked if he would want me to have an abortion if I accidentally became pregnant again right away. "And waste a perfectly good human being?" he said.

Coming to this quandary has been difficult for me. In fact, I believe the issue of abortion is difficult for all thoughtful people. I don't know anyone who has had an abortion who has not been haunted by it. If there is one thing I find intolerable about most of the so-called right-to-lifers, it is that they try to portray abortion rights as something that feminists thought up on a slow Saturday over a light lunch. That is nonsense. I also know that some people who support abortion rights are most comfortable with a monolithic position because it seems the strongest front against the smug and sometimes violent opposition.

10 But I don't feel all one way about abortion anymore, and I don't 10 think it serves a just cause to pretend that many of us do. For years I believed that a woman's right to choose was absolute, but now I wonder. Do I, with a stable home and marriage and sufficient stamina and money, have the right to choose abortion because a pregnancy is inconvenient right now? Legally I do have that right; legally I want always to have that right. It is the morality of exercising it under those circumstances that makes me wonder.

Technology has foiled us. The second trimester has become a time of resurrection; a fetus at six months can be one woman's late abortion, another's premature, viable child. Photographers now have film of embryos the size of a grape, oddly human, flexing their fingers, sucking their thumbs. Women have amniocentesis to find out whether they are carrying a child with birth defects that they may choose to abort. Before the procedure, they must have a sonogram, one of those fuzzy black-and-white photos like a love song heard through static on the radio, which shows someone is in there.

I have taped on my VCR a public-television program in which somehow, inexplicably, a film is shown of a fetus in utero scratching its face, seemingly putting up a tiny hand to shield itself from the camera's eye. It would make a potent weapon in the arsenal of the antiabortionists. I grow sentimental about it as it floats in the salt water, part fish, part human being. It is almost living, but not quite. It has almost turned my heart around, but not quite turned my head.

Questions on Meaning

1. Quindlen is not actually arguing for or against abortion. Is she arguing for anything at all, or merely describing how she feels? Explain your answer with evidence from the essay.
2. Although Quindlen admits she is pro-choice, she says she is actually somewhere "in the middle." Explain what that means. In what sense is she still pro-choice even while being in the middle?
3. The essay's last sentence helps us understand the mixed feelings about which Quindlen is writing. What does it mean to think one thing with your head and feel something else with your heart? How can these conflicting realities exist in an equilibrium?

Questions on Rhetorical Strategy and Style

1. Even though the essay is not primarily an argument for or against the right to an abortion, it does use some writing strategies of persuasion to argue its position "in the middle." Identify how she offers reasons why some women should have the right to have an abortion.
2. Quindlen uses several examples of situations in which abortion may or may not be appropriate. Analyze her examples. What makes her descriptions of the women in these situations effective?

Writing Assignments

1. Ask several friends—of both sexes—about how they feel about abortion. Try to go beyond the simple issue of legality or "rights"—how do they *feel* deep inside about it? Are ambiguity and conflicting feelings common? Do the men and women you talk to express different opinions? If so, can you account for the differences?
2. Quindlen differentiates between legality and morality on the issue of abortion. For example, murder is certainly illegal and to most people immoral. Suicide, however, is legal in some states (think of the debate about "assisted suicide" for people with terminal illness), though many argue it is immoral. What do you think about the distinction between the law and a moral sense of right and wrong? Should morality dictate legality? What problems might result if everything considered immoral or "wrong" were made illegal on that basis? Write an essay in which you discuss the

separation of law and morality. Be sure to use examples to clarify and support your thinking.

3. Choose a social issue currently being debated—gun control, human cloning, mandatory AIDS testing, pornography on the Internet, or any other topic about which people have strong feelings. Write a descriptive essay in which you present your thoughts and feelings about the topic, *not* arguing for or against a particular position on the issue. Make sure you still have a thesis that summarizes what you think and feel, even though you are not attempting to persuade the reader. Use examples, real or hypothetical, to clarify your thoughts and feelings.

The Sermon on the Mount

The Bible

The Bible has been translated into many different languages by many different authors. Varying versions have had different purposes at various times in history, so when a text comes from the Bible, it can differ greatly from another translation of the same text. The Bible was first collected into a canon (a group of works that are considered to be approved by authority) around the third century. That canon was written in Latin and was kept from the hands of common people for centuries. The text was read from the pulpit by priests and told as stories among those not literate in Latin. At the time of the Protestant revolution in the 1500s, a group of historical books were omitted from the Protestant canon so that the Protestant Bible has only sixty-six books. The Old Testament, or Hebrew scriptures, were originally written in Hebrew and then translated into Greek and finally Latin. The New Testament was written in Greek and Aramaic and is of more recent origin than the Hebrew scriptures. The Sermon on the Mount is perhaps the most famous of the preaching events chronicled in Matthew.

The Sermon on the Mount occurred after Jesus debated the wise and educated men in the city. He went out to the countryside to meditate and pray, but the people followed him even to his resting place. There he gave them a summary of his ideas and of his agenda for salvation.

Reprinted from *The King James Bible* (1611).

Matthew 5

And seeing the multitudes, he went up into a mountain: and when he was set, his disciples came unto him:

²And he opened his mouth, and taught them, saying,

³Blessed are the poor in spirit: for theirs is the kingdom of heaven.

⁴Blessed are they that mourn: for they shall be comforted.

⁵Blessed are the meek: for they shall inherit the earth.

⁶Blessed are they which do hunger and thirst after righteousness: for they shall be filled.

⁷Blessed are the merciful: for they shall obtain mercy.

⁸Blessed are the pure in heart: for they shall see God.

⁹Blessed are the peacemakers: for they shall be called the children of God.

¹⁰Blessed are they which are persecuted for righteousness' sake: for theirs is the kingdom of heaven.

¹¹Blessed are ye, when men shall revile you, and persecute you, and shall say all manner of evil against you falsely, for my sake.

¹²Rejoice, and be exceeding glad: for great is your reward in heaven: for so persecuted they the prophets which were before you.

¹³Ye are the salt of the earth: but if the salt have lost his savour, wherewith shall it be salted? it is thenceforth good for nothing, but to be cast out, and to be trodden under foot of men.

¹⁴Ye are the light of the world. A city that is set on a hill cannot be hid.

¹⁵Neither do men light a candle, and put it under a bushel, but on a candlestick; and it giveth light unto all that are in the house.

¹⁶Let your light so shine before men, that they may see your good works, and glorify your Father which is in heaven.

¹⁷Think not that I am come to destroy the law, or the prophets: I am not come to destroy, but to fulfil.

¹⁸For verily I say unto you, Till heaven and earth pass, one jot or one tittle shall in no wise pass from the law, till all be fulfilled.

¹⁹Whosoever therefore shall break one of these least commandments, and shall teach men so, he shall be called the least in the kingdom of heaven: but whosoever shall do and teach them, the same shall be called great in the kingdom of heaven.

²⁰For I say unto you, That except your righteousness shall exceed

the righteousness of the scribes and Pharisees, ye shall in no case enter into the kingdom of heaven.

²¹Ye have heard that it was said by them of old time, Thou shalt not kill; and whosoever shall kill shall be in danger of the judgment:

²²But I say unto you, That whosoever is angry with his brother without a cause shall be in danger of judgment: and whosoever shall say to his brother, Raca, shall be in danger of the council: but whosoever shall say, Thou fool, shall be in danger of hell fire.

²³Therefore if thou bring thy gift to the altar, and there rememberest that thy brother hath ought against thee;

²⁴Leave there thy gift before the altar, and go thy way; first be reconciled to thy brother, and then come and offer thy gift.

²⁵Agree with thine adversary quickly, whiles thou art in the way with him; lest at any time the adversary deliver thee to the judge, and the judge deliver thee to the officer, and thou be cast into prison.

²⁶Verily I say unto thee, Thou shalt by no means come out thence, till thou hast paid the uttermost farthing.

²⁷Ye have heard that it was said by them of old, Thou shalt not commit adultery:

²⁸But I say unto you, That whosoever looketh on a woman to lust after her hath committed adultery with her already in his heart.

²⁹And if thy right eye offend thee, pluck it out, and cast it from thee: for it is profitable for thee that one of thy members should perish, and not that thy whole body should be cast into hell.

³⁰And if thy right hand offend thee, cut it off, and cast it from thee: for it is profitable for thee that one of thy members should perish, and not that thy whole body should be cast into hell.

³¹It hath been said, Whosoever shall put away his wife, let him give her a writing of divorcement:

³²But I say unto you, That whosoever shall put away his wife, saving for the cause of fornication, causeth her to commit adultery: and whosoever shall marry her that is divorced committeth adultery.

³³Again, ye have heard that it hath been said by them of old time, Thou shalt not forswear thyself, but shalt perform unto the Lord thine oaths:

³⁴But I say unto you, Swear not at all; neither by heaven; for it is God's throne:

³⁵Nor by the earth; for it is his footstool: neither by Jerusalem; for it is the city of the great King.

³⁶Neither shalt thou swear by the head, because thou canst not make one hair white or black.

³⁷But let your communication be, Yea, yea; Nay, nay: for whatsoever is more than these cometh of evil.

³⁸Ye have heard that it hath been said, An eye for an eye, and a tooth for a tooth:

³⁹But I say unto you, That ye resist not evil: but whosoever shall smite thee on thy right cheek, turn to him the other also.

⁴⁰And if any man will sue thee at the law, and take away thy coat, let him have thy cloke also.

⁴¹And whosoever shall compel thee to go a mile, go with him twain.

⁴²Give to him that asketh thee, and from him that would borrow of thee turn not thou away.

⁴³Ye have heard that it hath been said, Thou shalt love thy neighbour, and hate thine enemy.

⁴⁴But I say unto you, Love your enemies, bless them that curse you, do good to them that hate you, and pray for them which despitefully use you, and persecute you;

⁴⁵That ye may be the children of your Father which is in heaven: for he maketh his sun to rise on the evil and on the good, and sendeth rain on the just and on the unjust.

⁴⁶For if ye love them which love you, what reward have ye? do not even the publicans the same?

⁴⁷And if ye salute your brethren only, what do ye more than others? do not even the publicans so?

⁴⁸Be ye therefore perfect, even as your Father which is in heaven is perfect.

Matthew 6

Take heed that ye do not your alms before men, to be seen of them: otherwise ye have no reward of your Father which is in heaven.

²Therefore when thou doest thine alms, do not sound a trumpet before thee, as the hypocrites do in the synagogues and in the synagogues and in the streets, that they may have glory of men. Verily I say unto you, They have their reward.

³But when thou doest alms, let not thy left hand know what thy right hand doeth:

[4]That thine alms may be in secret: and thy Father which seeth in secret himself shall reward thee openly.

[5]And when thou prayest, thou shalt not be as the hypocrites are: for they love to pray standing in the synagogues and in the corners of the streets, that they may be seen of men. Verily I say unto you, They have their reward.

[6]But thou, when thou prayest, enter into thy closet, and when thou hast shut thy door, pray to the Father which is in secret; and thy Father which seeth in secret shall reward thee openly.

[7]But when ye pray, use not vain repetitions, as the heathen do: for they think that they shall be heard for their much speaking.

[8]Be not ye therefore like unto them: for your Father knoweth what things ye have need of, before ye ask him.

[9]After this manner therefore pray ye: Our Father which art in heaven, Hallowed be thy name.

[10]Thy kingdom come. Thy will be done in earth, as it is in heaven.

[11]Give us this day our daily bread.

[12]And forgive us our debts, as we forgive our debtors.

[13]And lead us not into temptation, but deliver us from evil: For thine is the kingdom, and the power, and the glory, for ever. Amen.

[14]For if ye forgive men their trespasses, you heavenly Father will also forgive you:

[15]But if ye forgive not men their trespasses, neither will your Father forgive your trespasses.

[16]Moreover when ye fast, be not, as the hypocrites, of a sad countenance: for they disfigure their faces, that they may appear unto men to fast. Verily I say unto you, They have their reward.

[17]But thou, when thou fastest, anoint thine head, and wash thy face;

[18]That thou appear not unto men to fast, but unto thy Father which is in secret: and thy Father, which seeth in secret, shall reward thee openly.

[19]Lay not up for yourselves treasures upon earth, where moth and rust doth corrupt, and where thieves break through and steal:

[20]But lay up for yourselves treasures in heaven, where neither moth nor rust doth corrupt, and where thieves do not break through nor steal:

[21]For where your treasure is, there will your heart be also.

²²The light of the body is the eye: if therefore thine eye be single, thy whole body shall be full of light.

²³But if thine eye be evil, thy whole body shall be full of darkness. If therefore the light that is in thee be darkness, how great is that darkness!

²⁴No man can serve two masters: for either he will hate the one, and love the other; or else he will hold to the one, and despise the other. Ye cannot serve God and mammon.

²⁵Therefore I say unto you, Take no thought for your life, what ye shall eat, or what ye shall drink; nor yet for your body, what ye shall put on. Is not the life more than meat, and the body than raiment?

²⁶Behold the fowls of the air: for they sow not, neither do they reap, nor gather into barns; yet your heavenly Father feedeth them. Are ye not much better than they?

²⁷Which of you by taking thought can add one cubit unto his stature?

²⁸And why take ye thought for raiment? Consider the lilies of the field, how they grow; they toil not, neither do they spin:

²⁹And yet I say unto you, That even Solomon in all his glory was not arrayed like one of these.

³⁰Wherefore, if God so clothe the grass of the field, which to day is, and to morrow is cast into the oven, shall he not much more clothe you, O ye of little faith?

³¹Therefore take no thought, saying, What shall we eat? or, What shall we drink? or, Wherewithal shall we be clothed?

³²(For after all these things do the Gentiles seek:) for your heavenly Father knoweth that ye have need of all these things.

³³But seek ye first the kingdom of God, and his righteousness; and all these things shall be added unto you.

³⁴Take therefore no thought for the morrow: for the morrow shall take thought for the things of itself. Sufficient unto the day is the evil thereof.

Matthew 7

Judge not, that ye be not judged.

²For with what judgment ye judge, ye shall be judged: and with what measure ye mete, it shall be measured to you again.

³And why beholdest thou the mote that is in thy brother's eye, but considerest not the beam that is in thine own eye?

⁴Or how wilt thou say to thy brother, Let me pull out the mote out of thine eye; and, behold, a beam is in thine own eye?

⁵Thou hypocrite, first cast out the beam out of thine own eye; and then shalt thou see clearly to cast out the mote out of thy brother's eye.

⁶Give not that which is holy unto the dogs, neither cast ye your pearls before swine, lest they trample them under their feet, and turn again and rend you.

⁷Ask, and it shall be given you; seek, and ye shall find; knock, and it shall be opened unto you:

⁸For every one that asketh receiveth; and he that seeketh findeth; and to him that knocketh it shall be opened.

⁹Or what man is there of you, whom if his son ask bread, will he give him a stone?

¹⁰Or if he ask a fish, will he give him a serpent?

¹¹If ye then, being evil, know how to give good gifts unto your children, how much more shall your Father which is in heaven give good things to them that ask him?

¹²Therefore all things whatsoever ye would that men should do to you, do ye even so to them: for this is the law and the prophets.

¹³Enter ye in at the strait gate: for wide is the gate, and broad is the way, that leadeth to destruction, and many there be which go in thereat:

¹⁴Because strait is the gate, and narrow is the way, which leadeth unto life, and few there be that find it.

¹⁵Beware of false prophets, which come to you in sheep's clothing, but inwardly they are ravening wolves.

¹⁶Ye shall know them by their fruits. Do men gather grapes of thorns, or figs of thistles?

¹⁷Even so every good tree bringeth forth good fruit; but a corrupt tree bringeth forth evil fruit.

¹⁸A good tree cannot bring forth evil fruit, neither can a corrupt tree bringeth forth good fruit.

¹⁹Every tree that bringeth not forth good fruit is hewn down, and cast into the fire.

²⁰Wherefore by their fruits ye shall know them.

²¹Not every one that saith unto me, Lord, Lord, shall enter into the kingdom of heaven; but he that doeth the will of my Father which is in heaven.

[22]Many will say to me in that day, Lord, Lord, have we not prophesied in thy name? and in thy name have cast out devils? and in thy name done many wonderful works?

[23]And then will I profess unto them, I never knew you: depart from me, ye that work iniquity.

[24]Therefore whosoever heareth these sayings of mine, and doeth them, I will like him unto a wise man, which built his house upon a rock:

[25]And the rain descended, and the floods came, and the winds blew, and beat upon that house; and it fell not: for it was founded upon a rock.

[26]And every one that heareth these sayings of mine, and doeth them not, shall be likened unto a foolish man, which built his house upon the sand:

[27]And the rain descended, and the floods came, and the winds blew, and beat upon that house; and it fell: and great was the fall of it.

[28]And it came to pass, when Jesus had ended these sayings, the people were astonished at his doctrine:

[29]For he taught them as one having authority, and not as the scribes.

Questions on Meaning

1. Why is it better to be poor than rich in the economy of the Sermon on the Mount? What problems do rich people have that poor people do not? Where do the rich get their rewards?
2. Jesus says that one ought to love one's enemies. What kind of love is he talking about? How would you classify this love?
3. In this sermon, Jesus uses the example of taking a small piece of something from someone else's eye while not noticing the log in one's own eye. What kind of hypocrisy does this example describe? Why is it so easy to see faults in others?

Questions on Rhetorical Strategy and Style

1. Remember that Jesus has left the arguments in the city when he begins this sermon. Thus he begins his sermon by blessing those who are not rich, not learned, not self-indulgent, and not power-ful. Why does he move so easily to this beginning point? Does he show his human side in his choice?
2. This sermon is full of wonderful comparisons and contrasts. Note the way he contrasts the poor with the rich, the honest with the untruthful, the vengeful with the forgiving. How do these contrasting examples help to make his point clear to the people who have followed him into the mountains?
3. The final comparison in the sermon is the example of men who build their houses on rock versus those who build on sand. How does this powerful image bring to closure the points that Jesus has made in the sermon? What do you learn about the value of what you hold to be dear and important in life?

Writing Assignments

1. Describe ten things that are important to you. Consider what really matters, and which people are at the center of your life and experience. Where do you stand on Jesus' rejection of comfort and wealth? Why do you choose what you choose?
2. Read the sermon again. Make a chart of the examples that Jesus uses in the sermon. Using the chart, write an essay that traces the progression of his argument throughout the sermon. How does

the progression of examples emphasize what he wants to say to the people?

3. Write about the difference between powerful people you have encountered, and the less powerful people you have known. In what ways was Jesus right in his estimation of powerful and learned people, and in what ways might he have been unfair to them (if indeed you think that he was)?

The Ethic of Compassion

The Dalai Lama

His Holiness the Dalai Lama (1935–) was born a peasant in Taktser, Tibet under the birth name of Lhamo Dhondrub. He is the fourteenth Dalai Lama (spiritual leader of Tibet, reincarnation of the thirteenth Dalai Lama, and an incarnation of the Buddha of Compassion). He lives in Dharamsala, India. He was recognized at age two as the Dalai Lama and was enthroned on February 22, 1940. He completed the Geshe Lharampa Degree (equivalent to a Doctorate of Buddhist Philosophy) in 1959 and became head of Tibet—but was driven out by a Chinese invasion. He has worked on behalf of Tibet from India, asking the United Nations for help and working to bring Buddhist beliefs back to the country. He received the Albert Schweitzer Humanitarian Award (1987); Raoul Wallenberg Congressional Human Rights Award (1989); the Nobel Peace Prize (1989); Franklin D. Roosevelt Freedom Medal (1994); and the Hessian Peace Prize (2005). His books include Kindness, Clarity and Insight *(Snow Lion, 1984);* Compassion and the Individual *(Wisdom Publications, 1991); and* The Power of Compassion *(Harper Collins, 1995).*

Compassion is good when first considered, for it is easy to feel compassion for one who suffers. Compassion is harder to muster for wealthy and powerful people and even harder to feel when true compassion leads to a career change or an even greater life upheaval.

1 We noted earlier that all the world's major religions stress the importance of cultivating love and compassion. In the Buddhist philosophical tradition, different levels of attainment

are described. At a basic level, compassion (*nying je*) is understood mainly in terms of empathy—our ability to enter into and, to some extent, share others' suffering. But Buddhist—and perhaps others— believe that this can be developed to such a degree that not only does our compassion arise without any effort, but it is unconditional, undifferentiated, and universal in scope. A feeling of intimacy toward all other sentient beings, including of course those who would harm us, is generated, which is likened in the literature to the love a mother has for her only child.

But this sense of equanimity toward all others is not seen as an end in itself. Rather, it is seen as the springboard to a love still greater. Because our capacity for empathy is innate, and because the ability to reason is also an innate faculty, compassion shares the characteristics of consciousness itself. The potential we have to develop it is therefore stable and continuous. It is not a resource which can be used up—as water is used up when we boil it. And though it can be described in terms of activity, it is not like a physical activity which we train for, like jumping, where once we reach a certain height we can go no further. On the contrary, when we enhance our sensitivity toward others' suffering through deliberately opening ourselves up to it, it is believed that we can gradually extend out compassion to the point where the individual feels so moved by even the subtlest suffering of others that they come to have an over-whelming sense of responsibility toward those others. This causes the one who is compassionate to dedicate themselves entirely to helping others overcome both their suffering and the causes of their suffering. In Tibetan, this ultimate level of attainment is called *nying je chenmo,* literally "great compassion."

Now I am not suggesting that each individual must attain these advanced states of spiritual development in order to lead an ethically wholesome life. I have described *nying je chenmo* not because it is a precondition of ethical conduct but rather because I believe that pushing the logic of compassion to the highest level can act as a powerful inspiration. If we can just keep the aspiration to develop *nying je chenmo,* or great compassion, as an ideal, it will naturally have a significant impact on our outlook. Based on the simple recognition that, just as I do, so do all others desire to be happy and not to suffer, it will serve as a constant reminder against selfishness and partiality. It will remind us that there is little to be gained from being kind and generous because we hope to win something in return. It will remind us that actions motivated by the desire to create a good name for ourselves are still selfish, however much they may appear to be acts of kindness. It will also remind us that there is nothing exceptional about acts of charity toward those we already feel close to. And it will help us to recognize that the bias we naturally feel toward our families and friends is actually a highly unreliable thing on which to base ethical conduct. If we reserve ethical conduct for those whom we feel close to, the danger is that we will neglect our responsibilities toward those outside this circle.

Why is this? So long as the individuals in question continue to meet our expectations, all is well. But should they fail to do so, someone we consider a dear friend one day can become our sworn enemy the next. As we saw earlier, we have a tendency to react badly to all who threaten fulfillment of our cherished desires, though they may be our closest relations. For this reason, compassion and mutual respect offer a much more solid basis for our relations with others. This is also true of partnerships. If our love for someone is based largely on attraction, whether it be their looks or some other superficial characteristic, our feelings for that person are liable, over time, to evaporate. When they lose the quality we found alluring, or when we find ourselves no longer satisfied by it, the situation can change completely, this despite their being the same person. This is why relationships based purely on attraction are almost always unstable. On the other hand, when we begin to perfect our compassion, neither the other's appearance nor their behavior affects our underlying attitude.

Consider, too, that habitually our feelings toward others depend very much on their circumstances. Most people, when they see someone who is handicapped, feel sympathetic toward that person. But then when they see others who are wealthier, or better educated, or better placed socially, they immediately feel envious and competitive toward them. Our negative feelings prevent us from seeing the sameness of ourselves and all others. We forget that just like us, whether fortunate or unfortunate, distant or near, they desire to be happy and not to suffer.

The struggle is thus to overcome these feelings of partiality. Certainly, developing genuine compassion for our loved ones is the obvious and appropriate place to start. The impact our actions have on our close ones will generally be much greater than on others, and therefore our responsibilities toward them are greater. Yet we need to recognize that, ultimately, there are no grounds for discriminating in their favor. In this sense, we are all in the same position as a doctor confronted by ten patients suffering the same serious illness. They are each equally deserving of treatment. The reader should not suppose that what is being advocated here is a state of detached indifference, however. The further essential challenge, as we begin to extend our compassion toward all others, is to maintain the same level of intimacy as we feel toward those closest to us. In other words, what is being suggested is that we need to strive for even-handedness in our approach toward all others, a level ground into which we can plant the seed of *nying je chenmo,* of great love and compassion.

If we can begin to relate to others on the basis of such equanimity, our compassion will not depend on the fact that so and so is my husband, my wife, my relative, my friend. Rather, a feeling of closeness toward all others can be developed based on the simple recognition that, just like myself, all wish to be happy and to avoid suffering. In other words, we will start to relate to others on the basis of their sentient nature. Again, we can think of this in terms of an ideal, one which it is immensely difficult to attain. But, for myself, I find it one which is profoundly inspiring and helpful.

Let us now consider the role of compassionate love and kindheartedness in our daily lives. Does the ideal of developing it to the point where it is unconditional mean that we must abandon our own interests entirely? Not at all. In fact, it is the best way of serving them—indeed, it could even be said to constitute the wisest course for fulfilling self-interest. For if it is correct that those qualities such as love, patience, tolerance, and forgiveness are what happiness consists in, and if it is also correct that *nying je,* or compassion, as I have defined it, is both the source and the fruit of these qualities, then the more we are compassionate, the more we provide for our own happiness. Thus, any idea that concern for others, though a noble quality, is a matter for our private lives only, is simply short-sighted. Compassion belongs to every sphere of activity, including, of course, the workplace.

Here, though, I must acknowledge the existence of a perception—shared by many, it seems—that compassion is, if not actually an impediment, at least irrelevant to professional life. Personally, I would argue that not only is it relevant, but that when compassion is lacking, our activities are in danger of becoming destructive. This is because when we ignore the question of the impact our actions have on others' well-being, inevitably we end up hurting them. The ethic of compassion helps provide the necessary foundation and motivation for both restraint and the cultivation of virtue. When we begin to develop a genuine appreciation of the value of compassion, our outlook on others begins automatically to change. This alone can serve as a powerful influence on the conduct of our lives. When, for example, the temptation to deceive others arises, our compassion for them will prevent us from entertaining the idea. And when we realize that our work itself is in danger of being exploited to the detriment of others, compassion will cause us to disengage from it. So to take an imaginary case of a scientist whose research seems likely to be a source of suffering, they will recognize this and act accordingly, even if this means abandoning the project.

10   I do not deny that genuine problems can arise when we dedicate   10
ourselves to the ideal of compassion. In the case of a scientist who felt unable to continue in the direction their work was taking them, this could have profound consequences both for themselves and for their families. Likewise, those engaged in the caring professions—in medicine, counseling, social work, and so on—or even those looking after someone at home may sometimes become so exhausted by their duties that they feel overwhelmed. Constant exposure to suffering, coupled occasionally with a feeling of being taken for granted, can induce feelings of helplessness and even despair. Or it can happen that individuals may find themselves performing outwardly generous actions merely for the sake of it—simply going through the motions, as it were. Of course this is better than nothing. But when left unchecked, this can lead to insensitivity toward others' suffering. If this starts to happen, it is best to disengage for a short while and make a deliberate effort to reawaken that sensitivity. In this it can be helpful to remember that despair is never a solution. It is, rather, the ultimate failure. Therefore, as the Tibetan expression has it, even if the rope breaks nine times, we must splice it back together a tenth time. In this way, even if ultimately we do fail, at least there will be no feelings of regret. And when we combine this insight with a clear appreciation of our potential to benefit others, we find that we can begin to restore our hope and confidence.

Some people may object to this ideal on the grounds that by entering into others' suffering, we bring suffering on ourselves. To an extent, this is true. But I suggest that there is an important qualitative distinction to be made between experiencing one's own suffering and experiencing suffering in the course of sharing in others'. In the case of one's own suffering, given that it is involuntary, there is a sense of oppression: it seems to come from outside us. By contrast, sharing in someone else's suffering must at some level involve a degree of voluntariness, which itself is indicative of a certain inner strength. For this reason, the disturbance it may cause is considerably less likely to paralyze us than our own suffering.

Of course, even as an ideal, the notion of developing unconditional compassion is daunting. Most people, including myself, must struggle even to reach the point where putting others' interests on a par with our own becomes easy. We should not allow this to put us off, however. And while undoubtedly there will be obstacles on the way to developing a genuinely warm heart, there is the deep consolation of knowing that in doing so we are creating the conditions for our own happiness. As I mentioned earlier, the more we truly desire to benefit others, the greater the strength and confidence we develop and the greater the peace and happiness we experience. If this still seems unlikely, it is worth asking ourselves how else we are to do so. With violence and aggression? Of course not. With money? Perhaps up to a point, but no further. But with love, by sharing in others' suffering, by recognizing ourselves clearly in all others—especially those who are disadvantaged and those whose rights are not respected—by helping them to, be happy: yes. Through love, through kindness, through compassion we establish understanding between ourselves and others. This is how we forge unity and harmony.

Compassion and love are not mere luxuries. As the source both of inner and external peace, they are fundamental to the continued survival of our species. On the one hand, they constitute non-violence in action. On the other, they are the source of all spiritual qualities: of forgiveness, tolerance, and all the virtues. Moreover, they are the very thing that gives meaning to our activities and makes them constructive. There is nothing amazing about being highly educated; there is nothing amazing about being rich. Only when the individual has a warm heart do these attributes become worthwhile.

So to those who say that the Dalai Lama is being unrealistic in advocating this ideal of unconditional love, I urge them to experiment with it nonetheless. They will discover that when we reach beyond the confines of narrow self-interest, our hearts become filled with strength. Peace and joy become our constant companion. It breaks down barriers of every kind and in the end destroys the notion of my interest as independent from others' interest. But most important, so far as ethics is concerned, where love of one's neighbor, affection, kindness, and compassion live, we find that ethical conduct is automatic. Ethically wholesome actions arise naturally in the context of compassion.

Questions on Meaning

1. Compassion means to empathize with another, to feel that person's joy, pain, and hope. Why does the author say that feeling compassion for the disabled or the poor is easy? Why is it hard to feel sympathy for those we envy?
2. What would happen to our ordinary, selfish lives if we were to start feeling real compassion? Would we be able to use the environment and the rest of the world as we do now? What would we have to change?
3. What does the individual gain by feeling compassion? Is the kind of peace and love that are described in this essay really what people want? Why do most of us live lives that are aimed at making money and winning, rather than loving?

Questions on Rhetorical Strategy and Style

1. The tone of this essay is very gentle and kind, but the message is quite tough. How does the author warn the reader in the introduction that the essay is going to be demanding and maybe a bit disturbing?
2. The essay moves to a cause and effect structure: If one feels true compassion, the feeling may cause one to have to change one's life. The feeling, though a good one, may lead to uncomfortable results. How does this causality affect the reader of the essay? Is a reader likely to change behavior in light of this cause and effect explanation?
3. The end of the essay promises that great good can come from feeling compassion. How does the writer hope to persuade the reader that these benefits are worthwhile? Does this ending promise better things for the world if many readers are persuaded? Is it even possible?

Writing Assignments

1. A wise person once said that we should feel compassion rather than guilt, for we will act from compassion, but we will merely suffer from guilt. Think of someone you know whom you consider compassionate. Write about what that person does with life. What kind of work does the person do? What kind of entertainment and leisure activities does that person pursue?

2. Write about a world leader whom you consider compassionate. Show how this feeling is displayed in the person's actions. What would happen to world politics if everyone acted with compassion?
3. Consider a world conflict, either one occurring now or one in history. Write about how the events could be or would have been different had the parties shown more compassion and less aggression.

Address to the Prisoners in the Cook County Jail

Clarence Darrow

Clarence Darrow (1857–1938) was born in Kinsman, Ohio. Admitted to the bar in 1878, Darrow began his legal career as a small-town Ohio lawyer. In 1887, he moved to Chicago and began a successful practice in civil suits and labor law. Darrow rose to national prominence defending Eugene V. Debs and other union leaders in the 1894 Pullman strike. His notoriety grew with the Leob-Leopold kidnap, murder, and ransom case (1924) and with the case he is most often associated with today, the Scopes anti-evolution trial (1925), in which he argued against the politician and esteemed orator William Jennings Bryan. Darrow, who opposed capital punishment, often gave speeches on social and political issues. His books include Crime: Its Cause and Treatment *(1922). In this speech given to a group of prisoners, Darrow explains that they are in jail because they lack opportunity.*

1   If I looked at jails and crimes and prisoners in the way the ordinary person does, I should not speak on this subject to you. The reason I talk to you on the question of crime, its cause and cure, is that I really do not in the least believe in crime. There is no such thing as a crime as the word is generally understood. I do not believe there is any sort of distinction between the real moral conditions of the people in and out of jail. One is just as good as the other. The people here can no more help being here than the people outside can avoid being outside. I do not believe that people are in jail because they deserve to be. They are in jail simply because they cannot avoid it on account of circumstances which are entirely beyond their control and for which they are in no way responsible.

I suppose a great many people on the outside would say I was doing you harm if they should hear what I say to you this afternoon, but you cannot be hurt a great deal anyway, so it will not matter. Good people outside would say that I was really teaching you things that were calculated to injure society, but it's worth while now and then to hear something different from what you ordinarily get from preachers and the like. These will tell you that you should be good and then you will get rich and be happy. Of course we know that people do not get rich by being good, and that is the reason why so many of you people try to get rich some other way, only you do not understand how to do it quite as well as the fellow outside.

There are people who think that everything in this world is an accident. But really there is no such thing as an accident. A great many folks admit that many of the people in jail ought to be there, and many who are outside ought to be in. I think none of them ought to be here. There ought to be no jails; and if it were not for the fact that people on the outside are so grasping and heartless in their dealings with the people on the inside, there would be no such institution as jails.

I do not want you to believe that I think all you people here are angels. I do not think that. You are people of all kinds, all of you doing the best you can—and that is evidently not very well. You are people of all kinds and conditions and under all circumstances. In one sense everybody is equally good and equally bad. We all do the best we can under the circumstances. But as to the exact things for which you are sent here, some of you are guilty and did the particular act because you needed the money. Some of you did it because you are in the habit of doing it, and some of you because you are born to it, and it comes to be as natural as it does, for instance, for me to be good.

5   Most of you probably have nothing against me, and most of you would treat me the same way as any other person would, probably better than some of the people on the outside would treat me, because you think I believe in you and they know I do not believe in them. While you would not have the least thing against me in the world, you might pick my pockets. I do not think all of you would, but I think some of you would. You would not have anything against me, but that's your profession, a few of you. Some of the rest of you, if my doors were unlocked, might come in if you saw anything you wanted—not out of any malice to me, but because that is your trade. There is no doubt there are quite a number of people in this jail who

would pick my pockets. And still I know this—that when I get outside pretty nearly everybody picks my pocket. There may be some of you who would hold up a man on the street, if you did not happen to have something else to do, and needed the money; but when I want to light my house or my office the gas company holds me up. They charge me one dollar for something that is worth twenty-five cents. Still all these people are good people; they are pillars of society and support the churches, and they are respectable.

When I ride on the streetcars I am held up—I pay five cents for a ride that is worth two and a half cents, simply because a body of men have bribed the city council and the legislature, so that all the rest of us have to pay tribute to them.

If I do not want to fall into the clutches of the gas trust and choose to burn oil instead of gas, then good Mr. Rockefeller holds me up, and he uses a certain portion of his money to build universities and support churches which are engaged in telling us how to be good.

Some of you are here for obtaining property under false pretenses—yet I pick up a great Sunday paper and read the advertisements of a merchant prince—"Shirtwaists for 39 cents, marked down from $3.00."

When I read the advertisements in the paper I see they are all lies. When I want to get out and find a place to stand anywhere on the face of the earth, I find that it has all been taken up long ago before I came here, and before you came here, and somebody says, "Get off, swim into the lake, fly into the air; go anywhere, but get off." That is because these people have the police and they have the jails and the judges and the lawyers and the soldiers and all the rest of them to take care of the earth and drive everybody off that comes in their way.

A great many people will tell you that all this is true, but that it does not excuse you. These facts do not excuse some fellow who reaches into my pocket and takes out a five-dollar bill. The fact that the gas company bribes the members of the legislature from year to year, and fixes the law, so that all you people are compelled to be "fleeced" whenever you deal with them; the fact that the streetcar companies and the gas companies have control of the streets; and the fact that the landlords own all the earth—this, they say, has nothing to do with you.

Let us see whether there is any connection between the crimes of the respectable classes and your presence in the jail. Many of you people are in jail because you have really committed burglary; many of you, because you have stolen something. In the meaning of the law, you have taken some other person's property. Some of you have entered a store and carried off a pair of shoes because you did not have the price. Possibly some of you have committed murder. I cannot tell what all of you did. There are a great many people here who have done some of these things who really do not know themselves why they did them. I think I know why you did them—every one of you; you did these things because you were bound to do them. It looked to you at the time as if you had a chance to do them or not, as you saw fit; but still, after all, you had no choice. There may be people here who had some money in their pockets and who still went out and got some more money in a way society forbids. Now, you may not yourselves see exactly why it was you did this thing, but if you look at the question deeply enough and carefully enough you will see that there were circumstances that drove you to do exactly the thing which you did. You could not help it any more than we outside can help taking the positions that we take. The reformers who tell you to be good and you will be happy, and the people on the outside who have property to protect—they think that the only way to do it is by building jails and locking you up in cells on weekdays and praying for you Sundays.

I think that all of this has nothing whatever to do with right conduct. I think it is very easily seen what has to do with right conduct. Some so-called criminals—and I will use this word because it is handy, it means nothing to me—I speak of the criminals who get caught as distinguished from the criminals who catch them—some of these so-called criminals are in jail for their first offenses, but nine tenths of you are in jail because you did not have a good lawyer and, of course, you did not have a good lawyer because you did not have enough money to pay a good lawyer. There is no very great danger of a rich man going to jail.

Some of you may be here for the first time. If we would open the doors and let you out, and leave the laws as they are today, some of you would be back tomorrow. This is about as good a place as you can get anyway. There are many people here who are so in the habit of coming that they would not know where else to go. There are people who are born with the tendency to break into jail every chance they get, and they cannot avoid it. You cannot figure out your life and see why it was, but still there is a reason for it; and if we were all wise and knew all the facts, we could figure it out.

In the first place, there are a good many more people who go to jail in the wintertime than in the summer. Why is this? Is it because people are more wicked in winter? No, it is because the coal trust begins to get in its grip in the winter. A few gentlemen take possession of the coal, and unless the people will pay seven or eight dollars a ton for something that is worth three dollars, they will have to freeze. Then there is nothing to do but to break into jail, and so there are many more in jail in the winter than in summer. It costs more for gas in the winter because the nights are longer, and people go to jail to save gas bills. The jails are electric-lighted. You may not know it, but these economic laws are working all the time, whether we know it or do not know it.

15   There are more people who go to jail in hard times than in good   15
times—few people, comparatively, go to jail except when they are hard up. They go to jail because they have no other place to go. They may not know why, but it is true all the same. People are not more wicked in hard times. That is not the reason. The fact is true all over the world that in hard times more people go to jail than in good times, and in winter more people go to jail than in summer. Of course it is pretty hard times for people who go to jail at any time. The people who go to jail are almost always poor people—people who have no other place to live, first and last. When times are hard, then you find large numbers of people who go to jail who would not otherwise be in jail.

Long ago, Mr. Buckle, who was a great philosopher and historian, collected facts, and he showed that the number of people who are arrested increased just as the price of food increased. When they put up the price of gas ten cents a thousand, I do not know who will go to jail, but I do know that a certain number of people will go. When the meat combine raises the price of beef, I do not know who is going to jail, but I know that a large number of people are bound to go. Whenever the Standard Oil Company raises the price of oil, I know that a certain number of girls who are seamstresses, and who work night after night long hours for somebody else, will be compelled to go out on the streets and ply another trade, and I know that Mr. Rockefeller and his associates are responsible and not the poor girls in the jails.

First and last, people are sent to jail because they are poor. Sometimes, as I say, you may not need money at the particular time, but you wish to have thrifty forehanded habits, and do not always wait until you are in absolute want. Some of you people are perhaps plying the trade, the profession, which is called burglary. No man in his right senses will go into a strange house in the dead of night and prowl around with a dark lantern through unfamiliar rooms and take chances of his life, if he has plenty of the good things of the world in his own home. You would not take any such chances as that. If a man had clothes in his clothespress and beefsteak in his pantry and money in the bank, he would not navigate around nights in houses where he knows nothing about the premises whatever. It always requires experience and education for this profession, and people who fit themselves for it are no more to blame than I am for being a lawyer. A man would not hold up another man on the street if he had plenty of money in his own pocket. He might do it if he had one dollar or two dollars, but he wouldn't if he had as much money as Mr. Rockefeller has. Mr. Rockefeller has a great deal better hold-up game than that.

The more that is taken from the poor by the rich, who have the chance to take it, the more poor people there are who are compelled to resort to these means for a livelihood. They may not understand it, they may not think so at once, but after all they are driven into that line of employment.

There is a bill before the legislature of this state to punish kidnaping children with death. We have wise members of the legislature. They know the gas trust when they see it and they always see it—they can furnish light enough to be seen; and this legislature thinks it is going to stop kidnaping children by making a law punishing kidnapers of children with death. I don't believe in kidnaping children, but the legislature is all wrong. Kidnaping children is not a crime, it is a profession. It has been developed with the times. It has been developed with our modern industrial conditions. There are many ways of making money—many new ways that our ancestors knew nothing about. Our ancestors knew nothing about a billion-dollar trust; and here comes some poor fellow who has no other trade and he discovers the profession of kidnaping children.

20 This crime is born, not because people are bad; people don't kidnap other people's children because they want the children or because they are devilish, but because they see a chance to get some money out of it. You cannot cure this crime by passing a law punishing by death kidnapers of children. There is one way to cure it. There is one way to cure all these offenses, and that is to give the people a chance to live. There is no other way, and there never was any other way since the

world began; and the world is so blind and stupid that it will not see. If every man and woman and child in the world had a chance to make a decent, fair, honest living, there would be no jails and no lawyers and no courts. There might be some persons here or there with some peculiar formation of their brain, like Rockefeller, who would do these things simply to be doing them; but they would be very, very few, and those should be sent to a hospital and treated, and not sent to jail; and they would entirely disappear in the second generation, or at least in the third generation.

I am not talking pure theory. I will just give you two or three illustrations.

The English people once punished criminals by sending them away. They would load them on a ship and export them to Australia. England was owned by lords and nobles and rich people. They owned the whole earth over there, and the other people had to stay in the streets. They could not get a decent living. They used to take their criminals and send them to Australia—I mean the class of criminals who got caught. When these criminals got over there, and nobody else had come, they had the whole continent to run over, and so they could raise sheep and furnish their own meat, which is easier than stealing it. These criminals then became decent, respectable people because they had a chance to live. They did not commit any crimes. They were just like the English people who sent them there, only better. And in the second generation the descendants of those criminals were as good and respectable a class of people as there were on the face of the earth, and then they began building churches and jails themselves.

A portion of this country was settled in the same way, landing prisoners down on the southern coast; but when they got here and had a whole continent to run over and plenty of chances to make a living, they became respectable citizens, making their own living just like any other citizen in the world. But finally the descendants of the English aristocracy who sent the people over to Australia found out they were getting rich, and so they went over to get possession of the earth as they always do, and they organized land syndicates and got control of the land and ores, and then they had just as many criminals in Australia as they did in England. It was not because the world had grown bad; it was because the earth had been taken away from the people.

Some of you people have lived in the country. It's prettier than it is here. And if you have ever lived on a farm you understand that if you put a lot of cattle in a field, when the pasture is short they will jump over the fence; but put them in a good field where there is plenty of pasture, and they will be law-abiding cattle to the end of time. The human animal is just like the rest of the animals, only a little more so. The same thing that governs in the one governs in the other.

25   Everybody makes his living along the lines of least resistance. A   25
wise man who comes into a country early sees a great undeveloped land. For instance, our rich men twenty-five years ago saw that Chicago was small and knew a lot of people would come here and settle, and they readily saw that if they had all the land around here it would be worth a good deal, so they grabbed the land. You cannot be a landlord because somebody has got it all. You must find some other calling. In England and Ireland and Scotland less than five per cent own all the land there is, and the people are bound to stay there on any kind of terms the landlords give. They must live the best they can, so they develop all these various professions—burglary, picking pockets, and the like.

Again, people find all sorts of ways of getting rich. These are diseases like everything else. You look at people getting rich, organizing trusts and making a million dollars, and somebody gets the disease and he starts out. He catches it just as a man catches the mumps or the measles; he is not to blame, it is in the air. You will find men speculating beyond their means, because the mania of money-getting is taking possession of them. It is simply a disease—nothing more, nothing less. You cannot avoid catching it; but the fellows who have control of the earth have the advantage of you. See what the law is: when these men get control of things, they make the laws. They do not make the laws to protect anybody; courts are not instruments of justice. When your case gets into court it will make little difference whether you are guilty or innocent, but it's better if you have a smart lawyer. And you cannot have a smart lawyer unless you have money. First and last it's a question of money. Those men who own the earth make the laws to protect what they have. They fix up a sort of fence or pen around what they have, and they fix the law so the fellow on the outside cannot get in. The laws are really organized for the protection of the men who rule the world. They were never organized or enforced to do justice. We have no system for doing justice, not the slightest in the world.

Let me illustrate: Take the poorest person in this room. If the community had provided a system of doing justice, the poorest person in this room would have as good a lawyer as the richest, would he not? When you went into court you would have just as long a trial and just as fair a trial as the richest person in Chicago. Your case would not be tried in fifteen or twenty minutes, whereas it would take fifteen days to get through with a rich man's case.

Then if you were rich and were beaten, your case would be taken to the Appellate Court. A poor man cannot take his case to the Appellate Court; he has not the price. And then to the Supreme Court. And if he were beaten there he might perhaps go to the United States Supreme Court. And he might die of old age before he got into jail. If you are poor, it's a quick job. You are almost known to be guilty, else you would not be there. Why should anyone be in the criminal court if he were not guilty? He would not be there if he could be anywhere else. The officials have no time to look after all these cases. The people who are on the outside, who are running banks and building churches and making jails, they have no time to examine 600 or 700 prisoners each year to see whether they are guilty or innocent. If the courts were organized to promote justice the people would elect somebody to defend all these criminals, somebody as smart as the prosecutor—and give him as many detectives and as many assistants to help, and pay as much money to defend you as to prosecute you. We have a very able man for state's attorney, and he has many assistants, detectives, and policemen without end, and judges to hear the cases—everything handy.

Most all of our criminal code consists in offenses against property. People are sent to jail because they have committed a crime against property. It is of very little consequence whether one hundred people more or less go to jail who ought not to go—you must protect property, because in this world property is of more importance than anything else.

30   How is it done? These people who have property fix it so they can   30 protect what they have. When somebody commits a crime it does not follow that he has done something that is morally wrong. The man on the outside who has committed no crime may have done something. For instance: to take all the coal in the United States and raise the price two dollars or three dollars when there is no need of it, and thus kill thousands of babies and send thousands of people to the poorhouse and tens of thousands to jail, as is done every year in the United States—this is a greater crime than all the people in our jails ever committed; but the law does not punish it. Why? Because the fellows

who control the earth make the laws. If you and I had the making of the laws, the first thing we would do would be to punish the fellow who gets control of the earth. Nature put this coal in the ground for me as well as for them and nature made the prairies up here to raise wheat for me as well as for them, and then the great railroad companies came along and fenced it up.

Most all of the crimes for which we are punished are property crimes. There are a few personal crimes, like murder—but they are very few. The crimes committed are mostly those against property. If this punishment is right the criminals must have a lot of property. How much money is there in this crowd? And yet you are all here for crimes against property. The people up and down the Lake Shore have not committed crime; still they have so much property they don't know what to do with it. It is perfectly plain why these people have not committed crimes against property; they make the laws and therefore do not need to break them. And in order for you to get some property you are obliged to break the rules of the game. I don't know but what some of you may have had a very nice chance to get rich by carrying a hod for one dollar a day, twelve hours. Instead of taking that nice, easy profession, you are a burglar. If you had been given a chance to be a banker you would rather follow that. Some of you may have had a chance to work as a switchman on a railroad where you know, according to statistics, that you cannot live and keep all your limbs more than seven years, and you can get fifty dollars or seventy-five dollars a month for taking your lives in your hands; and instead of taking that lucrative position you chose to be a sneak thief, or something like that. Some of you made that sort of choice. I don't know which I would take if I was reduced to this choice. I have an easier choice.

I will guarantee to take from this jail, or any jail in the world, five hundred men who have been the worst criminals and law-breakers who ever got into jail, and I will go down to our lowest streets and take five hundred of the most abandoned prostitutes, and go out somewhere where there is plenty of land, and will give them a chance to make a living, and they will be as good people as the average in the community.

There is one remedy for the sort of condition we see here. The world never finds it out, or when it does find it out it does not enforce it. You may pass a law punishing every person with death for burglary, and it will make no difference. Men will commit it just the same. In

England there was a time when one hundred different offenses were punishable with death, and it made no difference. The English people strangely found out that so fast as they repealed the severe penalties and so fast as they did away with punishing men by death, crime decreased instead of increased; that the smaller the penalty the fewer the crimes.

Hanging men in our county jails does not prevent murder. It makes murderers.

35 And this has been the history of the world. It's easy to see how to 35 do away with what we call crime. It is not so easy to do it. I will tell you how to do it. It can be done by giving the people a chance to live—by destroying special privileges. So long as big criminals can get the coal fields, so long as the big criminals have control of the city council and get the public streets for streetcars and gas rights—this is bound to send thousands of poor people to jail. So long as men are allowed to monopolize all the earth, and compel others to live on such terms as these men see fit to make, then you are bound to get into jail.

The only way in the world to abolish crime and criminals is to abolish the big ones and the little ones together. Make fair conditions of life. Give men a chance to live. Abolish the right of private ownership of land, abolish monopoly, make the world partners in production, partners in the good things of life. Nobody would steal if he could get something of his own some easier way. Nobody will commit burglary when he has a house full. No girl will go out on the streets when she has a comfortable place at home. The man who owns a sweatshop or a department store may not be to blame himself for the condition of his girls, but when he pays them five dollars, three dollars, and two dollars a week, I wonder where he thinks they will get the rest of their money to live. The only way to cure these conditions is by equality. There should be no jails. They do not accomplish what they pretend to accomplish. If you would wipe them out there would be no more criminals than now. They terrorize nobody. They are a blot upon any civilization, and a jail is an evidence of the lack of charity of the people on the outside who make the jails and fill them with the victims of their greed.

Questions on Meaning

1. Darrow repeatedly states that jails should be done away with. What happens to "criminals" if there are no jails? What does he contend will happen to the crime rate if there are no jails? What evidence does he provide to support these beliefs?
2. Explain what Darrow means when he states that there are people born with the tendency to break *into* jail. Why does he say there are more people in jail in the winter than summer? When else do jails tend to fill up?
3. State Darrow's thesis in this speech in your own words. Explain why you do or do not agree with it.

Questions on Rhetorical Strategy and Style

1. How does Darrow compare and contrast the crimes of "criminals" with the crimes of people outside jails in terms of pickpocketing and holdups? How does he propose to "abolish crime and criminals"? Explain why you think his solution to crime would or would not work.
2. How does Darrow use a rhetorical strategy of cause and effect to explain why being poor and needy and without a bright future results in more people being in jail? Find other examples of cause and effect, such as the impact of strict punishment on the crime rate.
3. Throughout this essay, Darrow makes sardonic comments, such as "be good and then you will get rich and be happy" and "building jails and locking you up in cells on weekdays and praying for you Sundays" and "then they began building churches and jails themselves." What does this rhetorical strategy tell you about his feeling for the people "outside," the "good people"? Who are the wealthy and controlling people outside he castigates the most?

Writing Assignments

1. Explain why you agree or disagree with Darrow that almost all the people in jail are there because they cannot help it. What do you think would happen if 500 "men who have been the worst criminals" and 500 "abandoned prostitutes" were given land and a chance to make a living? Describe what you think this hypothetical community would be like 1, 5, and 10 years after it was set up.

2. Darrow repeatedly takes verbal swipes at "Rockefeller." Research the Rockefeller family and fortunes at the turn of the century. Whom was he referring to? Why did he hold this Rockefeller in such disdain? What controversies surrounded Rockefeller?

3. Write an essay in support of or opposition to capital punishment. In the essay, compare the rates of various crimes in states that have capital punishment with states that do not. What do you feel are deterrents to crime if not capital punishment?

The Prisoner's Dilemma

Stephen Chapman

*Born and raised in Texas, Stephen Chapman (1954–)
began his journalistic career at Harvard University, where
he served on the staff of the* Harvard Crimson. *After
graduating with honors in 1976, Chapman began writing and editing for* The New Republic *magazine. He has
also written for a variety of other publications, including*
Slate, Reason, *and* The Weekly Standard. *Chapman left*
The New Republic *to join the editorial staff of the*
Chicago Tribune *in 1981. His* Tribune *column on
national and international affairs is syndicated in newspapers across the United States, and he is often called upon
for political commentary by network and cable news, public television, and public radio. Chapman's work covers a
wide range of topics, including the national health care
debate, immigration policies, the Syrian uprising, and
Iran's nuclear program. In his blog, "Minority of One:
Solving the World's Problems One Post at a Time," Chapman promises readers "an independent, libertarian per-
spective beholden to no party, candidate or dogma." In this
1980 essay, originally published in* The New Republic,
*Chapman questions American condemnation of the bar-
baric nature of Islamic punishment in light of conditions
endured by prisoners in the United States.*

Reprinted by permission from the *New Republic*, March 8, 1990.

If the punitive laws of Islam were applied for only one year, all the devastating injustices would be uprooted. Misdeeds must be punished by the law of retaliation; cut off the hands of the thief; kill the murderers; flog the adulterous woman or man. Your concerns, your "humanitarian" scruples are more childish than reasonable. Under the terms of Koranic law, any judge fulfilling the seven requirements (that he have reached puberty, be a believer, know the Koranic laws perfectly, be just, and not be affected by amnesia, or be a bastard, or be of the female sex) is qualified to be a judge in any type of case. He can thus judge and dispose of twenty trials in a single day, whereas the Occidental justice may take years to argue them out.

—*from* Sayings of the Ayatollah Khomeni (*Bantam Books*)

1 One of the amusements of life in the modern West is the 1 opportunity to observe the barbaric rituals of countries that are attached to the customs of the dark ages. Take Pakistan, for example, our newest ally and client state in Asia. Last October President Zia, in harmony with the Islamic fervor that is sweeping his part of the world, revived the traditional Moslem practice of flogging law-breakers in public. In Pakistan, this qualified as mass entertainment, and no fewer than 10,000 law-abiding Pakistanis turned out to see justice done to 26 convicts. To Western sensibilities the spectacle seemed barbaric—both in the sense of cruel and in the sense of pre-civilized. In keeping with Islamic custom each of the unfortunates—who had been caught in prostitution raids the previous night and summarily convicted and sentenced—was stripped down to a pair of white shorts, which were painted with a red stripe across the buttocks (the target). Then he was shackled against an easel, with pads thoughtfully placed over the kidneys to prevent injury. The floggers were muscular, fierce-looking sorts—convicted murderers, as it happens—who paraded around the flogging platform in colorful loin-cloths. When the time for the ceremony began, one of the floggers took a running start and brought a five-foot stave down across the first victim's buttocks, eliciting screams from the convict and murmurs from the audience. Each of the 26 received from five to 15 lashes. One had to be carried from the stage unconscious.

Flogging is one of the punishments stipulated by Koranic law, which has made it a popular penological device in several Moslem countries, including Pakistan, Saudi Arabia, and, most recently, the ayatollah's Iran. Flogging, or *Tá zir*, is the general punishment prescribed for offenses that don't carry an explicit Koranic penalty. Some crimes carry automatic *hadd* punishments—stoning or scourging (a severe whipping) for illicit sex, scourging for drinking alcoholic beverages, amputation of the hands for theft. Other crimes—as varied as murder and abandoning Islam—carry the death penalty (usually carried out in public). Colorful practices like these have given the Islamic world an image in the West, as described by historian G.H. Jansen, "of blood dripping from the stumps of amputated hands and from the striped backs of malefactors, and piles of stones barely concealing the battered bodies of adulterous couples." Jansen, whose book *Militant Islam* is generally effusive in its praise of Islamic practices, grows squeamish when considering devices like flogging, amputation, and stoning. But they are given enthusiastic endorsement by the Koran itself.

Such traditions, we all must agree, are no sign of an advanced civilization. In the West, we have replaced these various punishments (including the death penalty in most cases) with a single device. Our custom is to confine criminals in prison for varying lengths of time. In Illinois, a reasonably typical state, grand theft carries a punishment of three to five years; armed robbery can get you from six to 30. The lowest form of felony theft is punishable by one to three years in prison. Most states impose longer sentences on habitual offenders. In Kentucky, for example, habitual offenders can be sentenced to life in prison. Other states are less brazen, preferring the more genteel sounding "indeterminate sentence," which allows parole boards to keep inmates locked up for as long as life. It was under an indeterminate sentence of one to 14 years that George Jackson served 12 years in California prisons for committing a $70 armed robbery. Under a Texas law imposing an automatic life sentence for a third felony conviction, a man was sent to jail for life last year because of three thefts adding up to less than $300 in property value. Texas also is famous for occasionally imposing extravagantly long sentences, often running into hundreds or thousands of years. This gives Texas a leg up on Maryland, which used to sentence some criminals to life plus a day— a distinctive if superfluous flourish.

The punishment *intended* by Western societies in sending their criminals to prison is the loss of freedom. But, as everyone knows, the actual punishment in most American prisons is of a wholly different order. The February 2 riot at New Mexico's state prison in Santa Fe, one of several bloody prison riots in the nine years since the Attica bloodbath, once again dramatized the conditions of life in an American prison. Four hundred prisoners seized control of the prison before dawn. By sunset the next day 33 inmates had died at the hands of other convicts and another 40 people (including five guards) had been seriously hurt. Macabre stories came out of prisoners being hanged, murdered with blowtorches, decapitated, tortured, and mutilated in a variety of gruesome ways by drug-crazed rioters.

5   The Santa Fe penitentiary was typical of most maximum-security facilities, with prisoners subject to overcrowding, filthy conditions, and routine violence. It also housed first-time, non-violent offenders, like check forgers and drug dealers, with murderers serving life sentences. In a recent lawsuit, the American Civil Liberties Union called the prison "totally unfit for human habitation." But the ACLU says New Mexico's penitentiary is far from the nation's worst.

That American prisons are a disgrace is taken for granted by experts of every ideological stripe. Conservative James Q. Wilson has criticized our "crowded, antiquated prisons that require men and women to live in fear of one another and to suffer not only deprivation of liberty but a brutalizing regimen." Leftist Jessica Mitford has called our prisons "the ultimate expression of injustice and inhumanity." In 1973 a national commission concluded that "the American correctional system today appears to offer minimum protection to the public and maximum harm to the offender." Federal courts have ruled that confinement in prisons in 16 different states violates the constitutional ban on "cruel and unusual punishment."

What are the advantages of being a convicted criminal in an advanced culture? First there is the overcrowding in prisons. One Tennessee prison, for example, has a capacity of 806, according to accepted space standards, but it houses 2300 inmates. One Louisiana facility has confined four and five prisoners in a single six-foot-by-six-foot cell. Then there is the disease caused by overcrowding, unsanitary conditions, and poor or inadequate medical care. A federal appeals court noted that the Tennessee prison had suffered frequent outbreaks of infectious diseases like hepatitis and tuberculosis. But the most distinctive element of American prison life is its constant violence. In his book *Criminal Violence, Criminal Justice*, Charles Silberman noted that in one Louisiana prison, there were 211 stabbings in only three years, 11 of them fatal. There were 15 slayings in a prison in Massachusetts between 1972 and 1975. According to a federal court, in Alabama's penitentiaries (as in many others), "robbery, rape, extortion, theft and assault are everyday occurrences."

At least in regard to cruelty, it's not at all clear that the system of punishment that has evolved in the West is less barbaric than the grotesque practices of Islam. Skeptical? Ask yourself: would you rather be subjected to a few minutes of intense pain and considerable public humiliation, or to be locked away for two or three years in a prison cell crowded with ill-tempered sociopaths? Would you rather lose a hand or spend 10 years or more in a typical state prison? I have taken my own survey on this matter. I have found no one who does not find the Islamic system hideous. And I have found no one who, given the choices mentioned above, would not prefer its penalties to our own.

The great divergence between Western and Islamic fashions in punishment is relatively recent. Until roughly the end of the 18th century, criminals in Western countries rarely were sent to prison. Instead they were subjected to an ingenious assortment of penalties. Many perpetrators of a variety of crimes simply were executed, usually by some imaginative and extremely unpleasant method involving prolonged torture, such as breaking on the wheel, burning at the stake, or drawing and quartering. Michel Foucault's book *Discipline and Punishment: The Birth of the Prison* notes one form of capital punishment in which the condemned man's "belly was opened up, his entrails quickly ripped out, so that he had time to see them, with his own eyes, being thrown on the fire; in which he was finally decapitated and his body quartered." Some criminals were forced to serve on slave galleys. But in most cases various corporal measures such as pillorying, flogging, and branding sufficed.

10   In time, however, public sentiment recoiled against these mea-   10
sures. They were replaced by imprisonment, which was thought to have two advantages. First, it was considered to be more humane. Second, and more important, prison was supposed to hold out the possibility of rehabilitation—purging the criminal of his criminality—something that less civilized punishments did not even aspire to. An 1854 report by inspectors of the Pennsylvania prison system illustrates the hopes nurtured by humanitarian reformers:

Depraved tendencies, characteristic of the convict, have been restrained by the absence of vicious association, and in the mild teaching of Christianity, the unhappy criminal finds a solace for an involuntary exile from the comforts of social life. If hungry, he is fed; if naked, he is clothed; if destitute of the first rudiments of education, he is taught to read and write; and if he has never been blessed with a means of livelihood, he is schooled in a mechanical art, which in after life may be to him the source of profit and respectability. Employment is not his toil nor labor, weariness. He embraces them with alacrity, as contributing to his moral and mental elevation.

Imprisonment is now the universal method of punishing criminals in the United States. It is thought to perform five functions, each of which has been given a label by criminologists. First, there is simple *retribution:* punishing the lawbreaker to serve society's sense of justice and to satisfy the victims' desire for revenge. Second, there is *specific deterrence:* discouraging the offender from misbehaving in the future. Third, general deterrence: using the offender as an example to discourage others from turning to crime. Fourth, *prevention:* at least during the time he is kept off the streets, the criminal cannot victimize other members of society. Finally, and most important, there is *rehabilitation:* reforming the criminal so that when he returns to society he will be inclined to obey the laws and able to make an honest living.

How satisfactorily do American prisons perform by these criteria? Well, of course, they do punish. But on the other scores they don't do so well. Their effect in discouraging future criminality by the prisoner or others is the subject of much debate, but the soaring rates of the last 20 years suggest that prisons are not a dramatically effective deterrent to criminal behavior. Prisons do isolate convicted criminals, but only to divert crime from ordinary citizens to prison guards and fellow inmates. Almost no one contends anymore that prisons rehabilitate their inmates. If anything, they probably impede rehabilitation by forcing inmates into prolonged and almost exclusive association with other criminals. And prisons cost a lot of money. Housing a typical prisoner in a typical prison costs far more than a stint at a top university. This cost would be justified if prisons did the job they were intended for. But it is clear to all that prisons fail on the very grounds—humanity and hope of rehabilitation—that caused them to replace earlier, cheaper forms of punishment.

The universal acknowledgement that prisons do not rehabilitate criminals has produced two responses. The first is to retain the hope of rehabilitation but do away with imprisonment as much as possible and replace it with various forms of "alternative treatment," such as psychotherapy, supervised probation, and vocational training. Psychiatrist Karl Menninger, one of the principal critics of American penology, has suggested even more unconventional approaches, such as "a new job opportunity or a vacation trip, a course of reducing exercises, a cosmetic surgical operation or a herniotomy, some night school courses, a wedding in the family (even one for the patient!), an inspiring sermon." The starry-eyed approach naturally has produced a backlash from critics on the right, who think that it's time to abandon the goal of rehabilitation. They argue that prisons perform an important service just by keeping criminals *off* the streets, and thus should be used with that purpose in mind.

So the debate continues to rage in all the same old ruts. No one, of course, would think of copying the medieval practices of Islamic nations and experimenting with punishments such as flogging and amputation. But let us consider them anyway. How do they compare with our American prison system in achieving the ostensible objectives of punishment? First, do they punish? Obviously they do, and in a uniquely painful and memorable way. Of course any sensible person, given the choice, would prefer suffering these punishments to years of incarceration in a typical American prison. But presumably no Western penologist would criticize Islamic punishments on the grounds that they are not barbaric enough. Do they deter crime? Yes, and probably more effectively than sending convicts off to prison. Now we read about a prison sentence in the newspaper, then think no more about the criminal's payment for his crimes until, perhaps, years later we read a small item reporting his release. By contrast, one can easily imagine the vivid impression it would leave to be wandering through a local shopping center and to stumble onto the scene of some poor wretch being lustily flogged. And the occasional sight of an habitual offender walking around with a bloody stump at the end of his arm no doubt also would serve as a forceful reminder that crime does not pay.

15 Do flogging and amputation discourage recidivism? No one 15 knows whether the scars on his back would dissuade a criminal from risking another crime, but it is hard to imagine that corporal mea-

sures could stimulate a higher rate of recidivism than already exists. Islamic forms of punishment do not serve the favorite new right goal of simply isolating criminals from the rest of society, but they may achieve the same purpose of making further crimes impossible. In the movie *Bonnie and Clyde*, Warren Beatty successfully robs a bank with his arm in a sling, but this must be dismissed as artistic license. It must be extraordinarily difficult, at the very least, to perform much violent crime with only one hand.

Do the medieval forms of punishment rehabilitate the criminal? Plainly not. But long prison terms do not rehabilitate either. And it is just as plain that typical Islamic punishments are no crueler to the convict than incarceration in the typical American state prison.

Of course there are other reasons besides its bizarre forms of punishment that the Islamic system of justice seems uncivilized to the Western mind. One is the absence of due process. Another is the long list of offenses—such as drinking, adultery, blasphemy, "profiteering," and so on—that can bring on conviction and punishment. A third is all the ritualistic mumbojumbo in pronouncements of Islamic law (like that talk about puberty and amnesia in the ayatollah's quotation at the beginning of this article). Even in these matters, however, a little cultural modesty is called for. The vast majority of American criminals are convicted and sentenced as a result of plea bargaining, in which due process plays almost no role. It has been only half a century since a wave of religious fundamentalism stirred this country to outlaw the consumption of alcoholic beverages. Most states also still have laws imposing austere constraints on sexual conduct. Only two weeks ago the *Washington Post* reported that the FBI had spent two and a half years and untold amounts of money to break up a nationwide pornography ring. Flogging the clients of prostitutes, as the Pakistanis did, does seem silly. But only a few months ago Mayor Koch of New York was proposing that clients caught in his own city have their names broadcast by radio stations. We are not so far advanced on such matters as we often like to think. Finally, my lawyer friends assure me that the rules of jurisdiction for American courts contain plenty of petty requirements and bizarre distinctions that would sound silly enough to foreign ears.

Perhaps it sounds barbaric to talk of flogging and amputation, and perhaps it is. But our system of punishment also is barbaric, and probably more so. Only cultural smugness about their system and willful ignorance about our own make it easy to regard the one as cruel and the other as civilized. We inflict our cruelties away from public view, while nations like Pakistan stage them in front of 10,000 onlookers. Their outrages are visible; ours are not. Most Americans can live their lives for years without having their peace of mind disturbed by the knowledge of what goes on in our prisons. To choose imprisonment over flogging and amputation is not to choose human kindness over cruelty, but merely to prefer that our cruelties be kept out of sight, and out of mind.

Public flogging and amputation may be more barbaric forms of punishment than imprisonment, even if they are not more cruel. Society may pay a higher price for them, even if they particular criminal does not. Revulsion against officially sanctioned violence and infliction of pain derives from something deeply ingrained in Western conscience, and clearly it is something admirable. Grotesque displays of the sort that occur in Islamic countries probably breed a greater tolerance for physical cruelty, for example, which prisons do not do precisely because they conceal their cruelties. In fact it is our admirable intolerance for calculated violence that makes it necessary for us to conceal what we have not been able to do away with. In a way this is a good thing, since it holds out the hope that we may eventually find a way to do away with it. But in another way it is a bad thing, since it permits us to congratulate ourselves on our civilized humanitarianism while violating its norms in this one area of our national life.

Questions on Meaning

1. Why did the West eventually abandon the kinds of corporal punishment still practiced in some Islamic countries? How does Chapman view that movement?

2. Why do you think that Chapman's respondents chose Islamic punishments over U.S. imprisonment, yet at the same time expressed horror at those punishments?

3. Chapman claims that the hidden nature of prison violence is at once a good thing and a bad thing. How does he explain this paradox, and how do you respond to it?

Questions on Rhetorical Strategy and Style

1. This essay's argument is presented in terms of comparison and contrast. Identify the key points of comparison between Western and Islamic forms of punishment and explain how they contribute to the effectiveness of Chapman's argument.

2. How does description function in this essay? Do you believe that the graphic descriptions of punishment are necessary? Why or why not?

3. How would the impact of the essay be altered if the Ayatollah Khomeni's words had been incorporated into the article rather than in an epigraph?

Writing Assignments

1. Conduct a survey based on Chapman's essay, explaining briefly the forms of Islamic punishment and the conditions in American prisons, and asking people their opinion of those punishments and which they would choose. Write a report on your findings, analyzing the responses. What do the responses reveal about American attitudes toward punishment of crime?

2. This essay was published in 1980. Gather information from sources such as the National Commission on Prison Abuse, the American Civil Liberties Union, and Human Rights Watch, and write a report on current conditions in American prisons. Have

conditions improved, deteriorated, or remained the same since Chapman's essay first appeared? How does your research reflect Chapman's conclusions?

Guarding Death's Door

John Cloud

Born in Evansville, Ind., John Cloud (1970–) grew up in Pine Bluff, Ark. He received a bachelor's degree in social studies from Harvard University and attended Oxford as a Rhodes Scholar. After college, Cloud interned at the Wall Street Journal *and the* Washington Post *before becoming a reporter for a free weekly paper in Washington, D.C. He joined the staff of* Time *magazine in 1997, where he writes for the Nation section, specializing in social issues. He has been second-place winner for both the National Headliner Award for feature writing and the Education Writers Association Prize. In this selection, Cloud explores the complex issues surrounding capital punishment by highlighting the story of a Texas prosecutor who proceeds very carefully before seeking the death penalty.*

1   On March 20, a man named Keith Clay died in Texas. His death was largely unremarkable except for one thing: he was the 300th person executed in Texas since the U.S. Supreme Court reauthorized capital punishment in 1976. One need not ignore the savagery of his crimes—prosecutors said Clay stood by while a friend murdered a father and his two kids on Christmas Eve 1993, 11 days before Clay himself butchered a store clerk—to pause at his execution.

Three hundred is an impressive milestone, not only because it exceeds the number of executions in the next five top death-penalty states combined, but also because it was reached so quickly. It took nearly two decades for Texas to consummate its first 100 death sentences after 1976—but only five more years to pass 200 and just three after that to hit 300. (The total has since climbed to 306.)

The approach of the 300th execution happened to coincide with a period of intense scrutiny of capital punishment. In January the departing Republican Governor of Illinois, George Ryan, delivered the biggest blow when he commuted the sentences of all 167 people who were to be executed in his state. "Our capital system is haunted by the demon of error," Ryan declared, "error in determining guilt and error in determining who among the guilty deserves to die." He and others argue that problems like racially motivated prosecutions, coerced confessions and unreliable witnesses have made the system capricious. Such worries may help explain why many states with capital punishment—there are 38 in all—seem to be wavering. The number of executions in the U.S., excluding Texas, fell to 38 last year from a peak of 63 in 1999.

Despite the high-profile second-guessing, most Americans favor capital punishment even though they don't fully trust the system that administers it. Not long before the 300th execution in Texas, a poll by the Scripps Howard Data Center found that three-quarters of Lone Star residents supported the death penalty. But a shocking 69% also said they believe the state has executed innocent people. National polls have generated similar results. In a Gallup poll released in May, 73% of the respondents said they thought at least one innocent had been put to death in the previous five years. Yet only about half of Americans favor a moratorium on executions to ensure that those on death row should be there. In other words, most of us believe the death-penalty system is broken—and we don't care.

5   Which means that if the system's flaws are to be fixed, they must   5 be fixed from within. And because prosecutors have great control over how a murder case is investigated and whether it deserves the death penalty, they will have to drive any meaningful reform. So where do you find a D.A. willing to both ignore public opinion and challenge his colleagues in the criminal-justice system? Surprisingly, in the heart of Texas.

The career of Travis County district attorney Ronald Earle coincides precisely with that of the modern death penalty. Earl was first elected D.A. in 1976, the year the Supreme Court reinstituted capital punishment. At the time, he enthusiastically backed the decision. "I thought it was too simple to talk about," he says in a clipped Texas cadence. But after prosecuting violent crime for a quarter-century, Earle doesn't believe capital punishment is so simple. To be sure, he still supports death for those few brutal murderers he believes would never stop killing, even in prison. And Earle can still summon the swagger of your typical TV district attorney. He says executing serial killer Kenneth McDuff, who is thought to have murdered at least 11 people, was "like shooting a rabid dog."

But like the rest of us, Earle has now watched broken souls walk free after years of wrongful incarceration; 56 have been released from death row in the past decade, either because they were deemed innocent or because of procedural mistakes, according to the Death Penalty Information Center. Unlike the rest of us, Earle still has to enforce the death penalty. He is often plagued by doubts when he must decide whether to seek death. "I agonize over it," he says. "There was a time when I thought the death penalty ought to have wider application, but my views have evolved." Today deciding whether to seek the death penalty is easily the hardest part of his job.

For a D.A., especially one from Texas, Earle is unusually vocal about his doubts. But many other prosecutors share his mix of philosophical support for the death penalty and nagging uncertainty about which cases are right for it. "When I first became prosecutor and had a death-penalty case, I looked forward to it . . . Now I get one and dread it," says Stanley Levco, who has been the prosecuting attorney in Vanderburgh County, Ind., since 1991. Levco strongly backs capital punishment, but he says capital cases take so long and cost so much that he wonders which ones are really worth it. "I tell this to the victim's family: there is an excellent chance this person will not die."

D.A.s have other concerns too. The National District Attorneys Association has called for DNA testing "At any stage of a criminal proceeding—even up to the eve of execution"—and stiff penalties for defense lawyers who don't adequately represent capital suspects. But Earle is going further. He is trying to do in his corner of Texas what death-penalty opponents say is impossible: enforce capital punishment flawlessly, ensuring that the innocent never spend a day on death row and the guilty are sent there only after trials free of bias and vengeance. Earle hopes that by raising every conceivable doubt about defendants before he decides to seek the death penalty for them, he can slay the "demon of error" invoked by Governor Ryan and achieve total certainty in the capital system.

10   It's a laudable goal. The trouble is, that's not his job. Jurors are   10
supposed to determine innocence, and judges are supposed to ensure

fairness. Most prosecutors feel an intense obligation to let the system work as it's built; crusading just isn't part of the prosecutorial gene pool. But Earle believes that, as he puts it, "the system cannot be trusted to run itself." It needs a watchdog, a backup.

Hence Earle has created virtually a second Travis County justice system for murder cases: well before any trial begins, he and his top lieutenants decide for themselves whether someone is guilty and deserves to die. If there's even a hint of doubt, they deny jurors the option of a death sentence. That approach has isolated Earle. Other D.A.s say he worries extravagantly over minor problems. Abolitionists have little use for him because he still sends people to die. But Earle's exertions raise an intriguing question: Does it take someone like him— someone who has more or less come to detest the death penalty—to save its credibility?

Ronnie Earle—even enemies call him Ronnie—is among the longest-serving D.A.s in the nation. He is also one of the most admired—and most controversial. Earle has been re-elected six times, and he can probably keep his job as long as he wants. His popularity doubtless owes something to the low crime rate in Austin, the county's biggest city (and state capital). In 2001, according to FBI figures, Austin had the fourth lowest per capita murder rate among U.S. cities with 500,000 to 1 million residents.

Earle's capital locale has extended his visibility beyond the county. He was one of the first prosecutors in Texas to create a victim-assistance program, in 1979; later he helped write a state law requiring every D.A. to open an office to connect crime victims with social services. He helped start Austin's Children's Advocacy Center, which works with abused kids, and a family-justice division of the D.A.'s office, which prosecutes those accused of domestic violence and helps their families get back to normal. A lot of prosecutors view such do-gooderism as a waste of time, preferring to devote themselves to cases guaranteed to go Live at 5. Earle, by contrast, rarely appears in court. He would rather attend, as he did recently, a conference in a motel ballroom off Highway 35 to talk about how to fight substance abuse. Predictably, those in the movement for community justice, which tries to combat the sources of crime as well as punish it, swoon over him. "He has a track record going back years of working toward crime prevention by working in the community," says Catherine Coles, a fellow at Harvard's Kennedy School of Government who studied Earle's office in the '90s.

He wasn't always so progressive. In the early '80s, when Reagan conservatism was ascendant, Earle sounded pretty much like any other law-and-order D.A. He spent a lot of time in court, and he stood out as a Democrat willing to aggressively prosecute corruption in his own party. (The G.O.P. didn't nominate a candidate to oppose Earle during the entire 1980s.) He seemed particularly conservative on the death penalty. In 1982 he said in a Limbaughesque radio commentary not only that he backed capital punishment but that it "reaffirms our humanity" and fulfills "our moral responsibility." He called it "society's right to self-defense."

15   But even back then, Earle felt more hesitant about the death   15 penalty than he let on. He had prosecuted only two death cases, and they had taken a lot out of him. Physically, capital cases require weeks if not months of work. More important, Earle found that his get-tough bravado afforded only weak protection against the emotional turbulence of a capital case. Working every day to ensure someone's death—even if he deserves it—can test one's humanity.

"At first, I thought justice was vengeance," he says, settling back into the chair in his second-floor office, which is not far from the pink-granite capitol. "D.A.s feel they have to give voice to the anguish that victims feel. And I tell you, that's a righteous anger. You look at these guys"—the killers, he means—"and some of them are monsters, just awful." Many prosecutors don't concern themselves with why they become awful, but Earle has a theory: "People learn to act through what I call the ethics infrastructure, that network of mommas and daddies and aunts and uncles and teachers and preachers"—he continues the list for some time—"who all teach us how to act. And that infrastructure has atrophied. When I was growing up"—Earle is 61 and was raised outside Fort Worth—"my mother had seven sisters and a brother. My dad had six siblings. So I had all these aunts and uncles plus my mother and father, and that structure is powerful. People don't have that now. And nobody is taking care of the children.

"So it's almost as if most of the people we send to death row, it's like we can say, 'Look what we made you do.' Most of them—if they had someone who had intervened in their life at an appropriate point, this would not have happened. And that's sad to realize. That doesn't necessarily make you squeamish about using the death penalty, but it does make you more discerning about it."

Earle has always been hard to pin down politically and culturally. He's not an unreconstructed liberal—and there are plenty of those in Austin—nor a conservative Democrat. He's an oddity. He grew up on a cattle ranch yet never eats beef. (Though when teased about that at a restaurant recently, Earle ordered the venison to show he would eat red meat.) He drives the beat-up pickup required for a Texas politician, but it's a Nissan. He has the scraggly hands of someone who broke several fingers playing football as a young man, but he has a deep fondness for academics. Three years ago, he and his wife Twila taught a University of Texas (UT) course earnestly titled "Re-Weaving the Fabric of Community."

His weak spot for intellectuals was evident in 1978, when he got his first death case. A young police officer, Ralph Ablanedo, had stopped a red Mustang for a traffic violation on a spring night. Prosecutors said the passenger, possibly fearing that the cop would find the drugs he was carrying, reached for his AK-47. Officer Ablanedo was shot several times (he was rushed to the hospital but died in surgery). A frantic chase ensued. The gunman, David Powell, fired at other officers but eventually surrendered to police.

20   Earle, who had been D.A. for less than 18 months, was pretty   20 green. When it came time to decide whether to seek death, he consulted Robert Kane, a UT philosophy professor. Kane has written extensively about how to encourage what he calls the moral sphere— "an ideal sphere in which everybody's rights to life, liberty and the pursuit of happiness are being respected," as Kane describes it. Sitting in Earle's home in the summer of 1978, he told the D.A. that sometimes, society must use the death penalty to send a message that it will protect people in vulnerable situations—people like cops alone on the walls. But, Kane told Earle gravely, "the burden is on you to show that no lesser punishment would do that job."

Earle took that burden seriously, and by the end of his second death case, also in 1978, he was worn out. The defendant was George Clark, who had abducted a young woman from Sears, raped her and stabbed her 38 times. Earle won a death sentence, but instead of trumpeting his victory, he gave a morose press conference calling it "a sad day for everybody." When a friend of the victim's brought him a congratulatory bottle of whiskey, Earle was aghast. "This is not a celebratory event," he scolded. Citing the administrative demands of running a large D.A.'s office and the talent of his staff prosecutors, Earle never again personally prosecuted a death case.

In the late '80s, Earle seemed to flirt with outright opposition to capital punishment. His office brought no death-penalty cases in 1988 or '89 and only one the following year. He took to telling people he was worried that capital punishment had become "a coarsening factor in the culture." Then along came Kenneth McDuff. Decades earlier, in the summer of 1966, McDuff and a friend abducted three teenagers— two boys and a girl. After robbing them, McDuff shot each boy in the head several times. Then he and his accomplice repeatedly raped the girl before crushing her throat with a broom (he was called the Broomstick Killer). Not surprisingly, he was sent to death row. But in 1972, when the Supreme Court ruled the U.S. death-penalty system unconstitutional, McDuff's sentence—like those of some 600 other death-row inmates across the U.S.—was commuted to life.

In 1989, as pressure mounted on prisons to relieve overcrowding, McDuff was paroled along with many other long-time inmates. He settled in Waco, Texas, and it wasn't long before young women in the area went missing. Authorities believe McDuff killed as many as eight before police finally caught on to him in 1992. Earle's office prosecuted McDuff for the murder of Colleen Reed, a 28-year-old accountant he had kidnapped from an Austin car wash, raped and killed. In 1994 McDuff was again sentenced to die, and he was executed four years later.

Earle says anyone who opposes capital punishment must grapple with the lessons of McDuff's case. "He was a clear and present danger," says Earle. "I guess a true [death penalty] abolitionist would say, 'Put this guy in prison for life,' but he had already gotten that punishment, and he got out. Also, murderers can kill again in prison. It happens all the time. The death penalty is a necessity in these cases."

By 2000, Earle seemed to have found a balance with capital punishment. He usually reserved it for the most gruesome murders, but that year he also sought it for Leonard Saldana, who had killed his ex-girlfriend. Death-penalty prosecutions in domestic-violence cases are rare, and rarely successful. Jurors can often be convinced that killing one's lover in a rage doesn't warrant execution. (Saldana got a life sentence. Earle later said he sought the death penalty partly because he wanted to send a message that he took domestic violence as seriously as any other crime.)

But just as the Saldana case was wrapping up, Earle learned that his office had mistakenly prosecuted two men for the 1988 murder of Nancy DePriest, a 20-year-old mother killed at the Pizza Hut where she worked. To Earle, it had seemed a horrific but fairly straightforward case: not long after the murder, a man named Christopher Ochoa, who worked at another Austin Pizza Hut, signed an intricately detailed confession. Ochoa said that he and a co-worker, Richard Danziger, had raped DePriest and that Ochoa then shot her in the head. The confession said the two had sexually violated her corpse and then washed it off in the restaurant bathroom.

Danziger denied the crime from Day One, but Ochoa's graphic confession helped convict them both. Partly because neither Danziger nor Ochoa had the violent criminal history typically needed to convince jurors of future dangerousness, Earle's office didn't seek the death penalty; the two were sentenced to life in prison. But in 1996 another Texas inmate, Achim Marino, started writing letters—to police, to the Austin *American-Statesman,* to Governor George W. Bush and eventually to the D.A.'s office—saying he had killed DePriest. Few believed him until 2000, when DNA tests revealed that Marino was in fact the sole killer.

One of Ochoa's attorneys, Keith Findley, says his client signed the confession only because police had threatened that he would get the death penalty if he didn't. Earle and assistant D.A. Claire Dawson-Brown, who worked on the case, say Ochoa may have been frightened in the police station, but they point out that he told the same story for years afterward. Nonetheless, two innocent men had been convicted—and one will pay for the rest of his life. In 1991 a fellow inmate wearing steel-toed shoes kicked Danziger in the head. Part of his brain had to be removed, and he now lives in a residential treatment facility in Jacksonville, Fla.

Earle was devastated. He felt awful for the victim's family, for Danziger and Ochoa, and, frankly, for himself. He told Bryan Case Jr., one of his most trusted assistant D.A.s, he was sure the Danziger-Ochoa debacle would mean the end of his political career. But instead of hunkering down, Earle admitted the system had screwed up. He asked Case to lead a task force to review hundreds of the office's old cases for any other errors. If an inmate still claimed innocence and if biological material from the crime still existed, prosecutors investigated further. Eventually they whittled down the list to seven inmates for whom new DNA tests might establish innocence. (None of the tests have been conducted yet because a new state law requires that the already overworked courts oversee the process of locating and testing biological material.)

30   After Danziger-Ochoa, Earle realized how lucky he had been that 30 he had not sought the death penalty against the men. He was more determined than ever to ensure that no innocent went to the death chamber—he couldn't live with himself if that happened. But is it possible to create a flawless system within a flawed one?

You might think that deciding whether to seek the death penalty is a simple matter of applying the facts of the case to the letter of the law. But capital statutes contain wide room for interpretation. To win a death sentence in Texas, for instance, prosecutors must first convince jurors "beyond a reasonable doubt" that a defendant is guilty of capital murder, which is an ordinary murder compounded by at least one of several aggravating factors, ranging from murdering someone you know is a cop to killing a child under 6. Second, the jury must find—again, beyond a reasonable doubt—that "there is a probability that the defendant would commit criminal acts of violence that would constitute a continuing threat to society."

      Consider the language. The prosecutor must erase any reasonable doubts that jurors can conjure not just about a past event but also about future ones. The latter presents an enormously tricky challenge for Earle's effort to achieve certainty, since no one can be sure about the future. In the face of that incertitude, many prosecutors punt: they seek the death penalty more often than not and allow jurors to determine whether the defendant is truly guilty and so dangerous that he must die., In the past decade, Earle has asked for the death penalty only 17 times out of a total of 63 capital-murder cases—27% of the time. (In Texas "capital" murder doesn't necessarily mean a death-penalty case; it's the designation for any aggravated murder, and prosecutors have full discretion in deciding whether to seek death in such cases.) By comparison, according to David Baldus of the University of Iowa, Philadelphia prosecutors seek the death penalty in about 70% of eligible cases. The figure is roughly 60% in Lincoln, Neb., and 45% in Georgia and New Jersey.

      In other words, if Earle wants moral certainty that no innocent is ever executed, other prosecutors want another kind of moral assurance—that most killers will get the maximum punishment possible. Appellate courts are left to sort out mistakes. Who's right? Actually, both are. According to Texas law, guilt and future dangerousness are matters for jurors, not prosecutors, to decide. Earle shouldn't shoulder responsibility for the entire system. But the U.S. Supreme Court has made clear that the prosecution's main job "is not that it shall win a case, but that justice shall be done." Texas has incorporated similar language into a law, one Earle often quotes.

Why can't we have it both ways? Why is it so hard to have a death penalty and make sure only the guilty receive it? Because of cases like *The State of Texas v. Delamora*. On Feb. 15, 2001, Travis County sheriff's deputy Keith Ruiz was shot and killed while prying open the door to Edwin Delamora's trailer. Ruiz had gone with members of the Capital Area Narcotics Task Force to arrest Delamora on charges of selling methamphetamine. Frightened, Delamora fired his 9-mm pistol through a window in his front door. Prosecutors said the bullet hit Ruiz in the aorta, killing him. Delamora claimed he fired because he thought he, his wife and his two kids were being robbed.

35 For Earle, it was a difficult case from the start. Because Ruiz was a 35 cop, people would expect a death-penalty prosecution. But Delamora did not have a criminally violent history, which weakened the argument for future dangerousness. On the other hand, a jury might be convinced that a meth dealer who had brazenly fired a pistol through his door had a propensity for violence. Earle remained undecided for months as staff prosecutors worked up the case. During that time, the narcotics task force conducted a second raid that ended in a fatality. And in yet another botched raid, members of the task force held several local residents at gunpoint while they searched their property for pot. They found only ragweed.

Earle has refused to speak publicly around the Delamora case, but associates in his town told me he knew what people were saying around town: those task-force guys were Rambo wannabes; it wasn't surprising that one of them had been shot. But no matter how aggressive the task force had been, it would be politically troublesome for Earle not to seek death for a cop killer. He looked forward to hearing what the death committee would recommend.

Formally called the Capital Murder Review Committee, the death committee is composed of 10 people from the D.A.'s office, most of them senior prosecutors, who hear the evidence in a case and then vote on whether Earle should seek the ultimate punishment. Their recommendation isn't binding—legally, only the D.A. can make the decision—but Earle always considers it carefully. "The amount of information in each case is enormous," says Case, the assistant D.A. "You're looking not only at the crime itself, the evidence there, but, in addition, a person's entire past life is opened for scrutiny . . . Maybe the guy was torturing cats when he was a kid." The death committee distills that material for Earle.

Characteristically, Earle picked an interesting mix for the committee. One member is Ellen Halbert, a nationally known victims' advocate who in 1986 was raped, stabbed, beaten in the head with a hammer and left for dead. The only nonlawyer on the committee, she is director of Earle's victim-witness division. Other members include Patricia Barrera, a devoutly Roman Catholic Latina who has a stained-glass cross affixed to her window and tries to reconcile her church's opposition to the death penalty with her duties as a prosecutor; Buddy Meyer, the gruff head of the trial division, who has a handlebar mustache and a picture of a Texas Ranger on his wall; and LaRu Woody, director of the family-justice division, who possesses a strong libertarian streak—she has a SMOKING PERMITTED sign in her office even though she doesn't smoke. First assistant D.A. Rosemary Lehmberg and five other veteran prosecutors round out the group.

The members met to consider the Delamora case several months before the trial, which was held last July. The death committee struggled with this question: Did Delamora know he was firing at a cop? Getting a capital-murder conviction would require proving he did. Meyer, the trial-division director, explains the reservations in the room this way: "The defendant was at home with his wife and children, and it was dark, and they were in the bedroom watching TV, and there was this loud banging on the side of their mobile home. The defendant felt there was evidence that these were people trying to break into his trailer and steal his dope and harm his family."

40 In the end, though, most members sided with the cops. Other 40 police officers at Delamora's trailer that night said they had clearly and repeatedly made their presence known. Barrera, the devout Catholic, voted against seeking death, as she usually does, but she was in the minority. Most people in the room went with their prosecutorial gut: "It's really difficult for prosecutors to be fully objective about cop killers," says assistant D.A. Case. "Some of us had doubts, and we

knew Ronnie would have to make an effort at resolving them in that particular case . . . I don't know everything that he was thinking when he made that one. I do know it was very hard."

It's likely that Earle went with his gut too. If he has any doubts, he doesn't seek death. He decided that the state would go ahead with its capital-murder case, relying on the jury to determine whether Delamora knew he was shooting at a police officer. But Earle knew jurors could never be dead sure about that, and he took death off the table. "We believe we have to look at it that they are guilty to a moral certainty, almost beyond any doubt whatsoever," says Case. "That's not the legal standard, but it's ours."

At the trial, the jury found Delamora guilty of capital murder, and because death wasn't an option, he automatically received what Texas law calls a "life" sentence in prison—no possibility of parole for 40 years. That wasn't enough for many Texans, who were furious: Ruiz's widow Bernadette and his boss, the county sheriff, were both quoted in the *American-Statesman* as criticizing the decision not to seek death. Texas attorney general John Cornyn, who was in the midst of a successful campaign to become a U.S. Senator, publicly attacked Earle. Nor was Delamora pleased; he is appealing.

In most other jurisdictions that enforce the death penalty, Delamora would be appealing from death row. And maybe that's not such a terrible thing. After all, at least since 1976, the creaky contraption that is the U.S. death-penalty system has worked, in the most narrow sense: it hasn't executed anyone who later turned out conclusively—through DNA evidence—to be innocent (although it should be noted that states haven't allowed DNA testing in all disputed executions).

Reformers like Earle hope that the capital system can promise something greater than merely preventing death at the last minute. It took someone like Earle to keep Delamora off death row—someone willing to ignore a grieving widow, the local sheriff and his own staff. Which makes Earle both courageous and freakish. It's one thing to understand that the vengeful emotions that accompany the death penalty can trump the factual certainties required to mete it out fairly. It's quite another to intellectualize the issue when a woman has lost her husband.

45   But Earle has always been a little weird. A close observer of Texas   45 politics e-mailed this description of him: "Thoughtful. Conspiratorial. Crusade. Half-whacked. Smart. Insightful. Wise. Nuts." Well, not

nuts. But most of it has a kernel of truth. Earle's reputation as conspiratorial derives largely from the workings of his office's public-integrity unit, a watchdog office that prosecutes those (including elected officials) who commit crimes in the course of their dealings with the state. Earle's job, in other words, is to root out conspiracies.

Earle is often suspected of bringing partisan cases on behalf of fellow Democrats. And while he has prosecuted 12 Democrats and only three Republicans, his biggest embarrassment came in 1994, after U.S. Senator Kay Bailey Hutchison, a prominent Republican, was indicted for allegedly using state employees to do political tasks. Earle amassed thousands of documents as evidence, and many thought the new Senator could lose her job. But at a pre-trial hearing, the judge and Earle clashed over the admissibility of the documents; fearing he would lose, Earle declined to present a case. Hutchison was quickly acquitted, and Earle was portrayed as a fool. Republicans have never quite forgiven him.

Like most other prosecutors, Earle often sees himself as an advocate—for his constituents, for the state, for crime victims. Because of their role, prosecutors tend to be portrayed in popular culture as modern-day knights. But Earle has come to prefer another metaphor. "I'm the gatekeeper," he says. "I don't dare ask my boss, the public, to sit in judgment of somebody that I don't think deserves to die. That's why they elect me, to exercise that judgment and not bother them." Buried in that philosophy is something radical—the notion that the jury system, as it's currently constructed, can't be trusted to send only the guilty to death row. Most prosecutors wouldn't embrace that philosophy, which is why it may take an Earle, not a knight, to slay the demon of error.

Questions on Meaning

1. Why have otherwise sympathetic public officials begun to question the legitimacy of capital punishment? What central issues concern these officials? Do you find these concerns valid? Explain your response.

2. Why does Ronnie Earle consider it necessary to examine the background of accused murderers? How do his reasons for this investigation differ from the reasons offered by opponents of capital punishment?

3. Earle's Capital Murder Review Committee is made up of people representing a diversity of views. How does this diversity help ensure fairness in investigating a case? How does it impede the work of the committee?

Questions on Rhetorical Strategy and Style

1. Why does Cloud open his article with background information on the death penalty in the United States? How does this background create a context for the story of Ronnie Earle?

2. Cloud uses several examples of death penalty cases. How are these cases similar? How are they different? What purpose does each example serve in helping the reader understand Earle's position?

3. According to Earle and others quoted in the article, the concept of capital punishment has specific effects on criminals and on society as a whole. What are those effects? Might those same effects be achieved without the death penalty?

Writing Assignments

1. Using the information in Cloud's article, write a profile of Ronnie Earle. Do not include details from the various cases cited in the article; instead, consider what the cases tell readers about Earle and incorporate that information into your profile.

2. Research the controversy surrounding Governor George Ryan's commutation of all death sentences in Illinois. Write a report on his action, including his rationale, the reaction to the decision, and the steps that have been taken to remedy the situation.

Jailhouse Talk

Laura Fraser

Born in Denver, Colo. Laura Fraser (1961–) received a bachelor of arts degree from Wesleyan University in 1982. Early in her career she was named Outstanding Young Journalist by the Northern California Society of Professional Journalists. Fraser's first book, Losing It: America's Obsession with Weight and the Industry that Feeds on It *(1997), was inspired in part by her own successful battle with bulimia. In 2003 she published* An Italianate Affair, *the account of her post-divorce trip to Italy. Critics praised the book, calling it a masterful combination of travelogue and memoir. Fraser has also written for a number of magazines, including* Vogue, Marie Claire, Bon Appetit, *and* The New York Times Magazine. *She has taught writing at several campuses of the University of California, and has spoken about the diet industry at a number of colleges and universities. In this selection, published in* Mother Jones, *Fraser tells the story of a gay ex-con's influential radio program that keeps inmates of Texas prisons in touch with their families and the outside world.*

1   Every Friday evening at nine, when the brick-red heat of an East Texas day starts to fade, Jon Buice lies on the narrow bed in his prison cell and turns on the radio. He stares at the ceiling with his headphones on, waiting for the sounds that will transport him, however briefly, beyond the walls that enclose him. Then he hears the buttermilk voice of Ray Hill, with his signature catcall: "Holler down the pipe chase and rattle them bars, 'cause we're gonna do a Prison Show."

Buice, 28, has been inside Texas prisons for the past 10 years; he's doing a 45-year stretch for murder. For eight of those years he has listened to the Prison Show every week, as do many of his fellow inmates in the Wynne Unit of the sprawling prison complex in Huntsville. The show, hosted by Ray Hill and broadcast from Pacifica's commercial-free KPFT station in Houston, reaches listeners all along the Gulf Coast, including 20 percent of the 145,000 inmates currently locked up in Texas. For the first hour, Hill, an ex-con who did time in Huntsville himself during the 1970s, reports on prison issues and interviews a wide variety of guests—parole board officers, wardens, substance abuse counselors, criminal defense attorneys. Hill is an outspoken activist who has the ear—and the phone number—of nearly everyone involved with the Texas prison system, and he doesn't hesitate to use those connections, whether it's to support parole for an individual inmate or to try to topple a corrupt prison official.

But while inmates like Buice listen to the first hour to hear news they otherwise can't get and to know there's someone sticking up for them on the outside, it's the second hour of the show they wait for. That's when the families and friends call in. *I love you,* the voices say. *Thanks for birthday card. Mom didn't start chemo yet, the hearing went well, we'll see you tomorrow.* Some callers just paint a picture of the world outside for people who are parched for scenery—*it's been real dry up here, and the grass is getting that burnt look.*

Hill banters with them, by turns offering sympathy for news of illness or death, engaging in small-town Texas talk ("Y'all have that watermelon festival going on this week?"), and goosing the prison system ("Any one of you in B wing who has actually received any kind of rehabilitation in prison, scream loud 'cause the warden's deaf"). Inmates in Texas aren't allowed to receive phone calls, except under rare circumstances, and some don't know how to read or write. In a state so big that some families can't afford to drive to see prisoners often, just listening to the voices of strangers on the Prison Show provides many inmates with their only sense of connection to the world beyond the prison walls. If you get a call yourself, Buice says, it's like hitting the jackpot. "Just for that split second, you're there with them," he says. "You're out in the world."

5   Through the thin but intimate connection of the airwaves, Hill 5 has created a kind of community on both sides of the razor wire—for inmates, and for the families outside who are doing time with them.

But he does more than talk on the radio; over the years Hill has managed to help rehabilitate individual prisoners. He visits prisoners regularly, speaking in recovery programs (he's been sober for 43 years) and mentoring inmates like Jon Buice. He urges them to avoid gangs, stay clean, and get some education, and he gives recent parolees a helping hand. "When inmates get released, often the first person they'll call is Ray," says Chuck Hurt, an ex-con who works for a parole attorney and books many of Hill's guests on the Prison Show. By gathering information directly from inmates, Hill has also helped expose prison scandals and spark statewide reforms, and the solid, no-nonsense information he offers on the air has earned him the grudging respect of prison officials and politicians across the state. "We have no problem with Ray Hill," says Larry Todd, spokesman for the Texas prison system. "That doesn't mean we agree with him on particular issues, but he gives accurate information and has expertise communicating with inmates—and that makes the show worthwhile."

Hill is an unlikely role model for hardened convicts. First off, he's openly gay, and as he puts it, "Being a punk in prison isn't low status—it's negative status." But he's outspoken about his sexual orientation, hoping it will create some tolerance for gay inmates on the inside. "If they don't like me being queer, they can go listen to the straight prison show," he says with a laugh, knowing that there isn't one. He's also tough enough to earn the respect of inmates—they know that, as a diabetic, he's suffered through having a toe and part of a leg amputated, and he's been through heart surgery, once doing the Prison Show from a hospital bed.

A graying, gristled bear at 61, Hill started the Prison Show 22 years ago, not long after he was released from prison. A former Baptist evangelist turned gay activist, Hill had co-founded KPFT, Houston's community radio station, in 1968—robbing warehouses on the weekends for his livelihood. "I specialized in something queens know something about," he says dryly, "antiques, art, jewels, and electronics." Caught in 1969 and sentenced to 20 consecutive eight-year sentences— that's 160 years—Hill managed, by some crafty jailhouse lawyering, to get out in just over four. But while he was inside, he listened to KPFT. "The station I helped create fed my head the whole time I was there."

Back on the outside, Hill decided to do a program that would speak to the inmates he left behind. The Prison Show started off as a ho-hum chat hour on prison politics. Then one day, a woman called from the roadside just minutes before airtime. "I could hear the traffic sounds—*whoosh, whoosh*—and this little tiny lady's voice full of anxiety, fear, and frustration," Hill recalls. The woman told him she'd saved for a long time to visit her son in prison, but she'd had an accident on the way, and would he please tell her son, because he listened to the show, that she wouldn't make it, but she loved him. Hill put her on the air. "Ma'am," he told her, in his courtly Texas drawl, "he's listening, so why don't you go ahead and tell him yourself." From that day on, the lines were jammed. "We call KPFT 'Keeping Prison Families Together,'" Hill says.

Before each show, Hill and his staff of volunteers gather around a conference table at the low-budget, volunteer-run station. Hill sorts through his mail, which is some measure of the show's popularity: Today he has 35 letters, and some weeks he gets as much as 25 pounds of mail. These days, the staff consists of two homeless ex-cons, a death penalty activist, and two women who married men in prison. Patsy Halanski, a Pentecostal who helps answer the phones, says she was a strict "lock 'em up and throw away the key" type before her son was imprisoned for aggravated robbery. At first, she refused to listen to Hill's show because he's an atheist and gay, but when she realized how much it meant to her son to hear her voice on the air, she eventually came down to the station. "I'd cry when kids would call in, saying, 'Daddy, I'm opening your present,'" she says, "and Ray—that big old goat—would wipe my tears."

10   This evening the show starts off with Hill interviewing Lon Bennett Glenn, a retired warden and author of *The Largest Hotel Chain in Texas*. Glenn is a hardened Marlboro Man, the kind you can imagine riding a horse in cotton fields full of inmates, as he did for many years. He looks uneasy next to Hill, who wears a T-shirt and a big opal pinkie ring, but they're cordial. They disagree on a lot of issues: Glenn supports the death penalty, and Hill is so opposed to it that he even showed up to protest the execution of a man who murdered one of his former lovers. Glenn thinks that educating convicts is a waste of taxpayer money, and Hill believes that it's the only hope. Still, they find common ground discussing the severe staffing shortage in Texas prisons—3,200 positions for guards remain unfilled across the state,

jeopardizing security—and both agree it's foolish to lock up drug users and other nonviolent offenders, who will just come out of prison much meaner than they went in.

Then it's time to open up the phones. A computer screen shows all seven lines full, with callers who have already been waiting for 40 minutes to get on the air. Over the next hour, Hill turns the airwaves over to some 30 callers. Rebecca Hernandez and her three young daughters elbow into the small studio—it's quicker for them to come in person than try to call. Her husband, "Tokyo," has been in prison for six years, serving three life sentences for "a drug deal gone bad," and his visiting privileges are limited. Hernandez comes every week. "The Prison Show has kept our relationship going," she says. One by one, her daughters, ages 4 to 10, take the microphone to tell Daddy they love him, and the youngest sings a whole verse of "You Are My Sunshine."

Hill also helps callers work the system, putting them in touch with attorneys, support groups, service agencies, and elected officials—and, when he needs to, raising seven kinds of hell with officials and the media. When one caller mentions that her home was searched by a sheriff and plainclothes police when her terrified 17-year-old daughter was home alone, Hill perks up. "Honey, why don't I give you my home phone number," he says. "This is the sort of thing I like to make an example of."

The calls from families, as well as letters from inmates and prison employees, are Hill's main source of information about goings-on in the prisons, which spur his activism. These days he's focused on medical problems, particularly the lack of care for prisoners with hepatitis C, an often-fatal liver disease that has reached epidemic proportions in some prisons. In the past, he has exposed inadequate treatment for prisoners with HIV, as well as wide discrepancies in how parole boards vote. "The Prison Show has broken a helluva lot more prison stories than the *Houston Chronicle*," says Randy Smith, a parole attorney. Smith and others credit Hill with uncovering the VitaPro scandal, in which former prison director James "Andy" Collins pushed through a $33 million contract to sell low-grade soymeal to the prisons in exchange for kickbacks. Inmates wrote to Hill about the scheme, and when newspapers took up the story, Collins resigned, and was indicted and convicted last year.

"Texas' theory about prisons is that if you're an inmate, you're like a mushroom—they're going to bury you underneath the ground and feed you shit," says Smith. "Consequently, inmates don't know a lot that goes on until the Prison Show tells them."

15   Hill shrugs off such praise, giving credit to the inmates who keep   15
him informed. "I'm minding my own business," he says, "and prisoners just feed me all kinds of valuable information."

On the inside, the Prison Show is sometimes too much for inmates to take. Most prisoners never get a call from friends or family. "The majority don't want to hear it at first," says Richard "Cowboy" Cain, a 45-year-old former inmate who spent 17 years in prison. "Most of us don't like pain, which is why we're there. When we go to prison we're separated from all the problems of family and financial responsibility, so then you've got this fool on the radio wanting to bring that back to us."

Cowboy, a former member of a white supremacist gang who wears a black hat, has two tattooed tears dripping from the corner of his eye, gang symbols commemorating two attempted "hits" he made on other inmates. He spent most of his time inside, he says, doing drugs and getting tattoos. Then he started listening to the Prison Show and noticed that it altered the dynamics of the gang inside the prison. "The head of the Muslim gang had the biggest radio, so we'd all gather around," he recalls. "When people were listening, you'd hear a black mama and a wife, and they weren't black anymore—they were just human." Cowboy began corresponding with Hill, and one day, when he was on the verge of being reassigned to maximum security after violating too many rules in a lower-security prison, he was sent to the warden's office, where he found Hill waiting. "You need to shut up and quit doing what you're doing," Hill told him. They struck up a friendship, and Hill helped steer him through drug and alcohol recovery. Hill bought him his first lunch in the free world, and invited him to work at the Prison Show—as long as he kept his act together.

"I'm a recovering alcoholic and ex-con—and so is Ray," says Cowboy. "He's been my mentor and friend, and he's been instrumental in keeping me out." Cowboy looks like he's about to shed some real tears over his tattooed ones. "Hell," he says, "he's like Mom."

"Mother Hill," as he sometimes calls himself, dishes a lot of advice to inmates. "The most important thing I do is to be a role model—not getting drunk, not stealing shit, not going back to prison, surviving, holding my head up, overcoming all that boot-mark-on-your-neck stuff," he says. A lot of inmates don't take his advice, and end up back inside. Hill hears a lot of false promises and gets burned a lot, but he's also seen some convicts turn their lives around.

20   One of those is Jon Buice. Sitting behind the mesh screen that 20 separates inmates from visitors at the Wynne Unit at Huntsville, Buice credits Hill with keeping him out of trouble in prison—even though Hill led the effort to put him behind bars in the first place. Buice was convicted of murder in 1992 for being part of a gang of 10 teenagers who beat a gay banker named Paul Broussard to death. When investigators were slow to respond to the event—as they had been to other violent crimes against gays—Hill organized a demonstration of 2,000 gay supporters on the Houston street corner where the murder occurred, putting the story on the front page and the evening news. Prosecutors and victims-rights advocates credit Hill with working for the conviction of all 10 teenagers. Buice, who had a knife, got the longest sentence—45 years. "Normally, I'm on the defense side," says Hill, "but this was a violent assault that resulted in a horrible death, and I owe it to the gay community to be concerned for their safety."

But once the "Woodlands 10" were in prison, Hill tried to get in touch with them. "You send people to prison for crimes against gays, they're going into an institution that is far more homophobic, where they'll be rewarded for doing violence against gay people," he says. "In addition to putting them in prison, you have to communicate with them." Hill contacted Buice through another inmate, and Buice found himself striking up a correspondence with the man who he says stirred up the media and put him behind bars. Hill encouraged him to go to school in prison, and Buice now has a college degree. With Hill's support, Buice also wrote an open letter of apology to the gay and lesbian community and attempted mediation with the victim's family. "It's ironic that we're friends," Buice says. "But he's the one who told me there's hope, and that people loved me, including him." Buice is up for parole next year, and Hill hopes he will take over as host of the Prison Show after he's released.

As Hill winds up his show this evening, he takes a moment to say hello to a few inmates he knows personally. He calls out to "Jon," telling him to hang in there. "Now we've just got to figure out a way to get you out of there," he says.

For the moment, listening to his friend, Buice is outside the red-brick walls of the prison. He imagines himself with a good job, and a family, and a place among the ex-cons who volunteer down at the station. Then he slips off his headphones and returns to reality, his 8-by-12-foot cell. But like other inmates who listen to the Prison Show each week, he is now measuring time not just in years, but in the days until next Friday night.

Questions on Meaning

1. How has Ray Hill's Prison Show "created a kind of community on both sides of the razor wire"? What characterizes this community?
2. Why is Hill respected by the prisoners who listen to him? Why do prison officials and politicians respect him? What is his appeal to each of these audiences?
3. How does Hill explain his decision to offer help to the "Woodlands 10"? To what extent do you agree or disagree with his reasoning? Explain your response.

Questions on Rhetorical Strategy and Style

1. In paragraph seven Fraser presents a detailed description of Ray Hill. What features of the man does she emphasize? How does this emphasis help readers understand Hill's appeal? If Fraser had chosen to present a simple physical description, how would the impact of the article be altered?
2. Cowboy Cain and Jon Buice are two examples of prisoners affected by Hill's program. How does each man represent a segment of Hill's audience? How do the specific features of each man's case illustrate Hill's influence?
3. Why do you think Fraser incorporates into her article brief narratives about the families of prisoners? What is the impact of these narratives on you as a reader?

Writing Assignments

1. In a brief essay, explain the impact of Ray Hill's Prison show—on prisoners, on their families, and on the prison system. Consider the following questions in your essay: Why should prisoners have an advocate like Hill? What are some of the positive results of his program? What negative results might there be?
2. Hill's Prison Show is especially valuable to children of prisoners. Research the various programs offered to help prisoners' families, particularly children. Write a report on one of these programs, focusing on its value to prisoners, their families, and society as a whole.

The New Colossus

Emma Lazarus

*Born to a wealthy sugar merchant in New York City,
Emma Lazarus (1849–1887) is considered the first significant Jewish-American writer.* Her first book, Poems
and Translations: Written Between the Ages Fourteen
and Sixteen *(1866), was praised by the celebrated tran-
scendentalist writer Ralph Waldo Emerson. During her
brief lifetime she published a number poetry collections
and translations, including* Admetus and Other Poems
(1871), Alide: An Episode of Goethe's Life *(1874),* The
Spagnoletto *(1876),* Poems and Ballads of Heinrich
Heine *(1881), and* Songs of a Semite: The Dance of
Death and Other Poems *(1882). In the early 1880s,
Lazarus became known as an outspoken reformer, respond-
ing to anti-Semitism at home and abroad, and to the
needs of immigrants. She was one of the first voices to urge
the establishment of a Jewish homeland in Palestine, and
she tirelessly worked for better working conditions for
newly arrived immigrants. In 1883 Lazarus was invited
to contribute a poem to the fundraising effort for the Statue
of Liberty. Her poem, printed here, was chosen as the
inscription for the statue's pedestal in 1903. In it she cele-
brates America's embracing of immigrants, focusing on the
strong, welcoming arms of the woman who would become
the symbol of the American Dream.*

Written for an art auction, "In Aid of the Bartholdi Pedestal Fund" in 1883.

1　　Not like the brazen giant of Greek fame,
　　　With conquering limbs astride from land to land;
　　　Here at our sea-washed, sunset gates shall stand
　　　A mighty woman with a torch, whose flame
5　　Is the imprisoned lightning, and her name
　　　Mother of Exiles. From her beacon-hand
　　　Glows world-wide welcome; her mild eyes command
　　　The air-bridged harbor that twin cities frame.
　　　"Keep, ancient lands, your storied pomp!" cries she
10　With silent lips. "Give me your tired, your poor,
　　　Your huddled masses yearning to breathe free,
　　　The wretched refuse of your teeming shore.
　　　Send these, the homeless, tempest-tost to me,
　　　I lift my lamp beside the golden door!"

Questions on Meaning

1. Why is it significant that the Statue of Liberty is a woman? How does Lazarus emphasize the feminine nature of the statue?
2. Lazarus calls the statue the "Mother of Exiles." What does this term mean to you? In what ways does this characterization emphasize the American Dream?

Questions on Rhetorical Strategy and Style

1. The title of Lazarus's poem refers to the Colossus of Rhodes, a great statue of the Greek sun god, built to celebrate the freedom and unity of Rhodes. Why do you think Lazarus uses this reference? How does she compare the Statue of Liberty to the Colossus? In what ways does she contrast the two?
2. What is the impact of the expression "wretched refuse"? Why would Lazarus use an image of trash to characterize those who seek refuge in the United States?

Writing Assignments

1. Write an essay analyzing the imagery in "The New Colossus." Focus on phrases such as "sea-washed, sunset gates," "imprisoned lightning," "silent lips," and others of your own choosing. Discuss the impact of these images on the "Questions on Meaning" of the poem.
2. The history of American immigration has not always reflected the words on the base of the Statue of Liberty. For example, at various times the country has seen strict and ethnic-based immigration quotas. Research immigration laws from the mid-nineteenth to the mid-twentieth centuries and focus on one bill that severely restricted immigration from one part of the world. Write an essay explaining the origins of the law, its impact on the country, and the forces that led to its being changed.
3. Since September 11, 2001, the federal government has used immigration laws to detain immigrants, particularly those from Islamic countries. While the government argues that these measures are necessary to preserve national security, civil libertarians

claim that they are violating the constitutional rights of detainees. Consult major newspapers and newsmagazines and research the arguments on both sides of the issue. Using references to experts to support your position, write an essay arguing for either the government's or the civil libertarians' position.

America and I

Anzia Yezierska

Known as the "sweatshop Cinderella," Anzia Yezierska (1880?–1970) was born Anzia Yeziersky in Poland. Her father, an Orthodox rabbi, brought the family to New York when Yezierska was around 10 years old. By the time she was 20, she had moved from her home to a settlement house for girls working in New York factories. Her hopes to escape a life of drudgery through education were raised when she earned a scholarship to Columbia University Teachers' College, but dashed when she realized that the only course open to her was domestic science (home economics). After graduating from Columbia she went on to attend—again on scholarship—the New York Academy of Dramatic Arts, and later to begin writing fiction based on her own experiences and those of other immigrant women. After two failed marriages and considerable frustration in getting her work published, Yezierska sought out the progressive philosopher of education John Dewey, who became her mentor and encouraged her to continue writing. Her short story "The Fat of the Land" was included in the Best Short Stories of 1919, *and her story collection* Hungry Hearts *was published in 1920. Throughout her career Yezierska sought to convey what she saw as the real story of American immigrants rather than the Hollywood rags-to-riches version. The following is one such story, in which Yezierska writes of a young immigrant's longing to shed the vestiges of the Old World and to become truly American.*

Reprinted from *America and I* (1922).

1   As one of the dumb, voiceless ones I speak. One of the millions   1
     of immigrants beating, beating out their hearts at your gates
     for a breath of understanding.

Ach! America! From the other end of the earth from where I came, America was a land of living hope, woven of dreams, aflame with longing and desire.

Choked for ages in the airless oppression of Russia, the Promised Land rose up—wings for my stifled spirit—sunlight burning through my darkness—freedom singing to me in my prison—deathless songs tuning prison-bars into strings of a beautiful violin.

I arrived in America. My young, strong body, my heart and soul pregnant with the unlived lives of generations clamoring for expression.

5   What my mother and father and their mother and father never   5
had a chance to give out in Russia, I would give out in America. The hidden sap of centuries would find release; colors that never saw light—songs that died unvoiced—romance that never had a chance to blossom in the black life of the Old World.

In the golden land of flowing opportunity I was to find my work that was denied me in the sterile village of my forefathers. Here I was to be free from the dead drudgery for bread that held me down in Russia. For the first time in America I'd cease to be a slave of the belly. I'd be a creator, a giver, a human being! My work would be the living joy of fullest self-expression.

But from my high visions, my golden hopes, I had to put my feet down on earth. I had to have food and shelter. I had to have the money to pay for it.

I was in America, among the Americans, but not of them. No speech, no common language, no way to win a smile of understanding from them, only my young, strong body and my untried faith. Only my eager, empty hands, and my full heart shining from my eyes!

God from the world! Here I was with so much richness in me, but my mind was not wanted without the language. And my body, unskilled, untrained, was not even wanted in the factory. Only one of two chances was left open to me: the kitchen, or minding babies.

10   My first job was as a servant in an Americanized family. Once,   10
long ago, they came from the same village from where I came. But they were so well-dressed, so well-fed, so successful in America, that they were ashamed to remember their mother tongue.

"What were to be my wages?" I ventured timidly, as I looked up to the well-fed, well-dressed "American" man and woman.

They looked at me with a sudden coldness. What have I said to draw away from me their warmth? Was it so low from me to talk of wages? I shrank back into myself like a low-down bargainer. Maybe they're so high up in well-being they can't any more understand my low thoughts for money.

From his rich height the man preached down to me that I must not be so grabbing for wages. Only just landed from the ship and already thinking about money when I should be thankful to associate with "Americans."

The woman, out of her smooth, smiling fatness assured me that this was my chance for a summer vacation in the country with her two lovely children. My great chance to learn to be a civilized being, to become an American by living with them.

So, made to feel that I was in the hands of American friends, invited to share with them their home, their plenty, their happiness, I pushed out from my head the worry for wages. Here was my first chance to begin my life in the sunshine, after my long darkness. My laugh was all over my face as I said to them: "I'll trust myself to you. What I'm worth you'll give me." And I entered their house like a child by the hand.

The best of me I gave them. Their house cares were my house cares. I got up early. I worked till late. All that my soul hungered to give I put into the passion with which I scrubbed floors, scoured pots, and washed clothes. I was so grateful to mingle with the American people, to hear the music of the American language, that I never knew tiredness.

There was such a freshness in my brains and such a willingness in my heart that I could go on and on—not only with the work of the house, but work with my head—learning new words from the children, the grocer, the butcher, the iceman. I was not even afraid to ask for words from the policeman on the street. And every new word made me see new American things with American eyes. I felt like a Columbus, finding new worlds through every new word.

But words alone were only for the inside of me. The outside of me still branded me for a steerage immigrant. I had to have clothes to forget myself that I'm a stranger yet. And so I had to have money to buy these clothes.

The month was up. I was so happy! Now I'd have money. *My own, earned* money. Money to buy a new shirt on my back—shoes on my feet. Maybe yet an American dress and hat!

20   Ach! How high rose my dreams! How plainly I saw all that I 20
would do with my visionary wages shining like a light over my head!

In my imagination I already walked in my new American clothes. How beautiful I looked as I saw myself like a picture before my eyes! I saw how I would throw away my immigrant rags tied up in my immigrant shawl. With money to buy—free money in my hands—I'd show them that I could look like an American in a day.

Like a prisoner in his last night in prison, counting the seconds that will free him from his chains, I trembled breathlessly for the minute I'd get the wages in my hand.

Before dawn I rose.

I shined up the house like a jewel-box.

25   I prepared breakfast and waited with my heart in my mouth for 25
my lady and gentleman to rise. At last I heard them stirring. My eyes were jumping out of my head to them when I saw them coming in and seating themselves by the table.

Like a hungry cat rubbing up to its boss for meat, so I edged and simpered around him as I passed them the food. Without my will, like a beggar, my hand reached out to them.

The breakfast was over. And no word yet from my wages.

"*Gottuniu!*"[1] I thought to myself. "Maybe they're so busy with their own things they forgot it's the day for my wages. Could they who have everything know what I was to do with my first American dollars? How could they, soaking in plenty, how could they feel the longing and the fierce hunger in me, pressing up through each visionary dollar? How could they know the gnawing ache of my avid fingers for the feel of my own, earned dollars? *My* dollars that I could spend like a free person. *My* dollars that would make me feel with everybody alike!"

Breakfast was long past.

30   Lunch came. Lunch past. 30

Oi-i weh! Not a word yet about my money.

It was near dinner. And not a word yet about my wages.

I began to set the table. But my head—it swam away from me. I broke a glass. The silver dropped from my nervous fingers. I couldn't stand it any longer. I dropped everything and rushed over to my American lady and gentleman.

"*Oi weh!* The money—my money—my wages!" I cried breathlessly.

35   Four cold eyes turned on me. 35

"Wages? Money?" The four eyes turned into hard stone as they looked me up and down. "Haven't you a comfortable bed to sleep, and three good meals a day? You're only a month here. Just came to America. And you already think about money. Wait till you're worth any money. What use are you without knowing English? You should be glad we keep you here. It's like a vacation for you. Other girls pay money yet to be in the country."

It went black for my eyes. I was so choked no words came to my lips. Even the tears went dry in my throat.

I left. Not a dollar for all my work.

For a long, long time my heart ached and ached like a sore wound. If murderers could have robbed me and killed me it wouldn't have hurt me so much. I couldn't think through my pain. The minute I'd see before me how they looked at me, the words they said to me— then everything began to bleed in me. And I was helpless.

40   For a long, long time the thought of ever working in an "Ameri-   40 can" family made me tremble with fear, like the fear of wild wolves. No—never again would I trust myself to an "American" family, no matter how fine their language and how sweet their smile.

It was blotted out in me all trust in friendship from "Americans." But the life in me still burned to live. The hope in me still craved to hope. In darkness, in dirt, in hunger and want, but only to live on!

There had been no end to my day—working for the "American" family.

Now rejecting false friendships from higher-ups in America, I turned back to the Ghetto. I worked on a hard bench with my own kind on either side of me. I knew before I began what my wages were to be. I knew what my hours were to be. And I knew the feeling of the end of the day.

From the outside my second job seemed worse than the first. It was in a sweatshop of a Delancey Street basement, kept up by an old, wrinkled woman that looked like a black witch of greed. My work was sewing on buttons. While the morning was still dark I walked into a dark basement. And darkness met me when I turned out of the basement.

45   Day after day, week after week, all the contact I got with America   45 was handling dead buttons. The money I earned was hardly enough to pay for bread and rent. I didn't have a room to myself. I didn't even have a bed. I slept on a mattress on the floor in a rat-hole of a room occupied by a dozen other immigrants. I was always hungry—oh, so

hungry! The scant meals I could afford only sharpened my appetite for real food. But I felt myself better off than working in the "American" family, where I had three good meals a day and a bed to myself. With all the hunger and darkness of the sweatshop, I had at least the evening to myself. And all night was mine. When all were asleep, I used to creep up on the roof of the tenement and talk out my heart in silence to the stars in the sky.

"Who am I? What am I? What do I want with my life? Where is America? Is there an America? What is this wilderness in which I'm lost?"

I'd hurl my questions and then think and think. And I could not tear it out of me, the feeling that America must be somewhere, somehow—only I couldn't find it—*my America*, where I would work for love and not for a living. I was like a thing following blindly after something far off in the dark!

"Oi weh!" I'd stretch out my hand up in the air. "My head is so lost in America! What's the use of all my working if I'm not in it? Dead buttons is not me."

Then the busy season started in the shop. The mounds of buttons grew and grew. The long day stretched out longer. I had to begin with the buttons earlier and stay with them till later in the night. The old witch turned into a huge greedy maw for wanting more and more buttons.

50   For a glass of tea, for a slice of herring over black bread, she   50
would buy us up to stay another and another hour, till there seemed no end to her demands.

One day, the light of self-assertion broke into my cellar darkness.

"I don't want the tea. I don't want your herring," I said with terrible boldness. "I only want to go home. I only want the evening to myself!"

"You fresh mouth, you!" cried the old witch. "You learned already too much in America. I want no clock-watchers in my shop. Out you go!"

I was driven out to cold and hunger. I could no longer pay for my mattress on the floor. I no longer could buy the bite in the mouth. I walked the streets. I knew what it is to be alone in a strange city, among strangers.

55   But I laughed through my tears. So I learned too much already in   55
America because I wanted the whole evening to myself? Well America has yet to teach me still more: how to get not only the whole evening to myself, but a whole day a week like the American workers.

That sweat-shop was a bitter memory but a good school. It fitted me for a regular factory. I could walk in boldly and say I could work at something, even if it is was only sewing on buttons.

Gradually, I became a trained worker. I worked in a light, airy factory, only eight hours a day. My boss was no longer a sweater and a blood-squeezer. The first freshness of the morning was mine. And the whole evening was mine. All day Sunday was mine.

Now I had better food to eat. I slept on a better bed. Now, I even looked dressed up like the American-born. But inside of me I knew that I was not yet an American. I choked with longing when I met an American-born, and I could say nothing.

Something cried dumb in me. I couldn't help it. I didn't know what it was I wanted. I only knew I wanted. I wanted. Like the hunger in the heart that never gets food.

60 An English class for foreigners started in our factory. The teacher had such a good, friendly face, her eyes looked so understanding, as if she could see right into my heart. So I went to her one day for an advice:

"I don't know what is with me the matter," I began. "I have no rest in me. I never yet done what I want."

"What is it you want to do, child?" she asked me.

"I want to do something with my head, my feelings. All day long, only with my hands I work."

"First you must learn English." She patted me as if I was not yet grown up. "Put your mind on that, and then we'll see."

65 So for a time I learned the language. I could almost begin to think with English words in my head. But in my heart the emptiness still hurt. I burned to give, to give something, to do something, to be something. The dead work with my hands was killing me. My work left only hard stones on my heart.

Again I went to our factory teacher and cried out to her: "I know already to read and write the English language, but I can't put it into words what I want. What is it in me so different that can't come out?"

She smiled at me down from her calmness as if I were a little bit out of my head. "What *do you want* to do?"

"I feel. I see. I hear. And I want to think it out. But I'm like dumb in me. I only feel I'm different—different from everybody."

She looked at me close and said nothing for a minute. "You ought to join one of the social clubs of the Women's Association," she advised.

"What's the Women's Association?" I implored greedily.

"A group of American women who are trying to help the working-girl find herself. They have a special department for immigrant girls like you."

I joined the Women's Association. On my first evening there they announced a lecture: "The Happy Worker and His Work," by the Welfare director of the United Mills Corporation.

"Is there such a thing as a happy worker at his work?" I wondered. "Happiness is only by working at what you love. And what poor girl can ever find it to work at what she loves? My old dreams about my America rushed through my mind. Once I thought that in America everybody works for love. Nobody has to worry for a living. Maybe this welfare man came to show me the *real* America that till now I sought in vain.

With a lot of polite words the head lady of the Women's Association introduced a higher-up that looked like the king of kings of business. Never before in my life did I ever see a man with such a sureness in his step, such power in his face, such friendly positiveness in his eye as when he smiled upon us.

"Efficiency is the new religion of business," he began. "In big business houses, even in up-to-date factories, they no longer take the first comer and give him any job that happens to stand empty. Efficiency begins at the employment office. Experts are hired for the one purpose, to find out how best to fit the worker to his work. It's economy for the boss to make the worker happy." And then he talked a lot more on efficiency in educated language that was over my head.

I didn't know exactly what it meant—efficiency—but if it was to make the worker happy at his work, then that's what I had been looking for since I came to America. I only felt from watching him that he was happy by his job. And as I looked on this clean, well-dressed, successful one, who wasn't ashamed to say he rose from an office-boy, it made me feel that I, too, could lift myself up for a person.

He finished his lecture, telling us about the Vocational-Guidance Center that the Women's Association started.

The very next evening I was at the Vocational-Guidance Center. There I found a young, college-looking woman. Smartness and health shining from her eyes! She, too, looked as if she knew her way in America. I could tell at the first glance: here is a person that is happy by what she does.

"I feel you'll understand me," I said right away.

She leaned over with pleasure in her face: "I hope I can."

"I want to work by what's in me. Only, I don't know what's in me. I only feel I'm different."

She gave me a quick, puzzled look from the corner of her eyes. "What are you doing now?"

"I'm the quickest shirtwaist hand on the floor. But my heart wastes away by such work. I think and think, and my thoughts can't come out."

"Why don't you think out your thoughts in shirtwaists? You could learn to be a designer. Earn more money."

"I don't want to look on waists. If my hands are sick from waists, how could my head learn to put beauty into them?"

"But you must earn your living at what you know, and rise slowly from job to job."

I looked at her office sign: "Vocational Guidance." "What's your vocational guidance?" I asked. "How to rise from job to job—how to earn more money?"

The smile went out from her eyes. But she tried to be kind yet. "What *do* you want?" she asked, with a sigh of last patience.

"I want America to want me."

She fell back in her chair, thunderstruck with my boldness. But yet, in a low voice of educated self-control, she tried to reason with me:

"You have to *show* that you have something special for America before America has need of you."

"But I never had a chance to find out what's in me, because I always had to work for a living. Only, I feel it's efficiency for America to find out what's in me so different, so I could give it out by my work."

Her eyes half closed as they bored through me. Her mouth opened to speak, but no words came from her lips. So I flamed up with all that was choking in me like a house on fire:

"America gives free bread and rent to criminals in prison. They got grand houses with sunshine, fresh air, doctors and teachers, even for the crazy ones. Why don't they have free boarding-schools for immigrants—strong people—willing people? Here you see us burning up with something different, and America turns her head away from us."

95   Her brows lifted and dropped down. She shrugged her shoulders 95
away from me with the look of pity we give to cripples and hopeless
lunatics.

"America is no Utopia. First you must become efficient in earning
a living before you can indulge in your poetic dreams."

I went away from the vocational-guidance office with all the air
out of my lungs. All the light out of my eyes. My feet dragged after
me like dead wood.

Till now there had always lingered a rosy veil of hope over my
emptiness, a hope that a miracle would happen. I would open up my
eyes some day and suddenly find the America of my dreams. As a
young girl hungry for love sees always before her eyes the picture of
lover's arms around her, so I saw always in my heart the vision of
Utopian America.

But now I felt that the America of my dreams never was and
never could be. Reality had hit me on the head as with a club. I felt
that the America that I sought was nothing but a shadow—an echo—
a chimera of lunatics and crazy immigrants.

100   Stripped of all illusion, I looked about me. The long desert of 100
wasting days of drudgery stared me in the face. The drudgery that I
had lived through, and the endless drudgery still ahead of me rose
over me like a withering wilderness of sand. In vain were all my cry-
ings, in vain were all frantic efforts of my spirit to find the living
waters of understanding for my perishing lips. Sand, sand was everywhere. With every seeking, every reaching out I only lost myself
deeper and deeper in a vast sea of sand.

I knew now the American language. And I knew now, if I talked
to the Americans from morning till night, they could not understand
what the Russian soul of me wanted. They could not understand *me*
any more than if I talked to them in Chinese. Between my soul and
the American soul were worlds of difference that no words could
bridge over. What was that difference? What made the Americans so
far apart from me?

I began to read the American history. I found from the first pages
that America started with a band of Courageous Pilgrims. They had
left their native country as I had left mine. They had crossed an
unknown ocean and landed in an unknown country, as I.

But the great difference between the first Pilgrims and me was
that they expected to make America, build America, create their own
world of liberty. I wanted to find it ready made.

I read on. I delved deeper down into the American history. I saw how the Pilgrim Fathers came to a rocky desert country, surrounded by Indian savages on all sides. But undaunted, they pressed on—through danger—through famine, pestilence, and want—they pressed on. They did not ask the Indians for sympathy, for understanding. They made no demands on anybody, but on their own indomitable spirit of persistence.

105 And I—I was forever begging a crumb of sympathy, a gleam of 105 understanding from strangers who could not sympathize, who could not understand.

I, when I encountered a few savage Indian scalpers, like the old witch of the sweat-shop, like my "Americanized" countryman, who cheated me of my wages—I, when I found myself on the lonely, untrodden path through which all seekers of the new world must pass, I lost heart and said: "There is no America!"

Then came a light—a great revelation! I saw America—a big idea—a deathless hope—a world still in the making. I saw that it was the glory of America that it was not yet finished. And I, the last comer, had her share to give, small or great, to the making of America, like those Pilgrims who came in the *Mayflower*.

Fired up by this revealing light, I began to build a bridge of understanding between the American-born and myself. Since their life was shut out from such as me, I began to open up my life and the lives of my people to them. And life draws life. In only writing about the Ghetto I found America.

Great chances have come to me. But in my heart is always a deep sadness. I feel like a man who is sitting down to a secret table of plenty, while his near ones and dear ones are perishing before his eyes. My very joy in doing the work I love hurts me like secret guilt, because all about me I see so many with my longings, my burning eagerness, to do and to be, wasting their days in drudgery they hate, merely to buy bread and pay rent. And America is losing all that richness of the soul.

110 The Americans of to-morrow, the America that is every day 110 nearer coming to be, will be too wise, too open-hearted, too friendly-handed, to let the least last-comer at their gates knock in vain with his gifts unwanted.

End Note

1. Oh, my God! (Yiddish)

Questions on Meaning

1. What hopes does Yezierska's narrator bring with her to America? What obstacles does she face in realizing those hopes? To what extent are the obstacles within her, and to what extent are they outside her?
2. What does the narrator mean when she says "I want America to want me"? Why does she continue to feel frustrated in this desire?
3. What lesson does the narrator learn from her study of the Pilgrims? How does she make use of that lesson?

Questions on Rhetorical Strategy and Style

1. How do the opening lines of the story help to establish the narrator's character? How would you describe her character?
2. What steps does the narrator envision as necessary in the process of becoming American? List those steps, and explain why she fails to achieve her goal by taking those steps.
3. How would you describe the tone of this narrative? What techniques does Yezierska use (e.g., word choice, images, figurative language) to establish the tone?

Writing Assignments

1. Yezierska's story can be considered a coming-of-age narrative in which the main character moves from innocence to experience. Write your own coming-of-age narrative, focusing on a time in your life when you shed naïve ideas and faced a harsher reality.
2. The narrator places great weight on the importance of learning English. Currently, the idea of English as an official language is the subject of much controversy. Research the issue and write an essay outlining the various positions regarding the English-only movement, concluding with your own position.

Why People Don't Help in a Crisis

John M. Darley and Bibb Latané

John M. Darley (1938–) graduated from Swarthmore College (1960) and Harvard University (M.A. 1962, Ph.D. 1965). He has done extensive work in psychology and philosophy and is an expert in research. His awards include a National Science Foundation fellowship (1961–1964), a Center for Advanced Study in the Behavioral Sciences fellowship (1985–1986), and a Guggenheim fellowship (1990–1991). His publications include Psychology *(multiple editions, Prentice Hall);* The Unresponsive Bystander: Why Doesn't He Help?, *with Bibb Latané (1970);* Justice, Liability, and Blame: Community Views and the Criminal Law, *with Paul H. Robinson;* Social Influences on Ethical Behavior in Organizations, *with David M. Messick and Tom R. Tyler. With Bibb Latané, he won the American Association for the Advancement of Science Socio-Psychological Essay Prize (1968) and Appleton-Century Crafts Manuscript Prize. He is Dorman T. Warren Professor of Psychology and Public Affairs at Princeton University.*

Bibb Latane (1937–) graduated from Yale University (1958) and University of Minnesota (Ph.D. 1963). He is a social psychologist who has worked extensively on bystander psychology with John Darley. His work on social loafing and other group behavior is also notable. He won the AAAS Prize for Behavioral Science Research, (1980), with Stephen G. Harkins and Kipling D. Williams, for "Many Hands Make Light the Work: Causes and Consequences of Social Loafing"; and with John M. Darley,

American Association for the Advancement of Science Socio-Psychological Essay Prize (1968) and Appleton-Century Crafts Manuscript Prize. His publications include The Unresponsive Bystander: Why Doesn't He Help?, *with John M. Darley (1970).*

In this article, the authors contend that people do care about one another, but fear often keeps them from acting. Also, groups tend to react much more slowly than individual people, so that one person might run to help whereas those in a group might hesitate as they wait for someone to lead.

1 Kitty Genovese is set upon by a maniac as she returns home from work at 3 A.M. Thirty-eight of her neighbors in Kew Gardens, N.Y., come to their windows when she cries out in terror; not one comes to her assistance, even though her assailant takes half an hour to murder her. No one so much as calls the police. She dies.

Andrew Mormille is stabbed in the head and neck as he rides in a New York City subway train. Eleven other riders flee to another car as the 17-year-old boy bleeds to death; not one comes to his assistance, even though his attackers have left the car. He dies.

Eleanor Bradley trips and breaks her leg while shopping on New York City's Fifth Avenue. Dazed and in shock, she calls for help, but the hurrying stream of people simply parts and flows past. Finally, after 40 minutes, a taxi driver stops and helps her to a doctor.

How can so many people watch another human being in distress and do nothing? Why don't they help?

5 Since we started research on bystander responses to emergencies, we have heard many explanations for the lack of intervention in such cases. "The megalopolis in which we live makes closeness difficult and leads to the alienation of the individual from the group," says the psychoanalyst. "This sort of disaster," says the sociologist, "shakes the sense of safety and sureness of the individuals involved and causes psychological withdrawal." "Apathy," says others. "Indifference."

All of these analyses share one characteristic: they set the indifferent witness apart from the rest of us. Certainly not one of us who reads about these incidents in horror is apathetic, alienated or depersonalized.

Certainly these terrifying cases have no personal implications for us. We needn't feel guilty, or re-examine ourselves, or anything like that. Or should we?

If we look closely at the behavior of witnesses to these incidents, the people involved begin to seem less inhuman and a lot more like the rest of us. They were not indifferent. The 38 witnesses of Kitty Genovese's murder, for example, did not merely look at the scene once and then ignore it. They continued to stare out of their windows, caught, fascinated, distressed, unwilling to act but unable to turn away.

Why, then, didn't they act?

There are three things the bystander must do if he is to intervene in an emergency: *notice* that something is happening; *interpret* that event as an emergency; and decide that he has *personal responsibility* for intervention. As we shall show, the presence of other bystanders may at each stage inhibit his action.

The Unseeing Eye

10 Suppose that a man has a heart attack. He clutches his chest, staggers 10 to the nearest building and slumps sitting to the sidewalk. Will a passerby come to his assistance? First, the bystander has to notice that something is happening. He must tear himself away from his private thoughts and pay attention. But Americans consider it bad manners to look closely at other people in public. We are taught to respect the privacy of others, and when among strangers we close our ears and avoid staring. In a crowd, then, each person is less likely to notice a potential emergency than when alone.

Experimental evidence corroborates this. We asked college students to an interview about their reactions to urban living. As the students waited to see the interviewer, either by themselves or with two other students, they filled out a questionnaire. Solitary students often glanced idly about while filling out their questionnaires: those in groups kept their eyes on their own papers.

As part of the study, we staged an emergency: smoke was released into the waiting room through a vent. Two thirds of the subjects who were alone noticed the smoke immediately, but only 25 percent of those waiting in groups saw it as quickly. Although eventually all the subjects did become aware of the smoke—when the atmosphere grew so smoky as to make them cough and rub their eyes—this study indicates that the more people present, the slower an individual may be to perceive an emergency and the more likely he is not to see it at all.

Seeing Is Not Necessarily Believing

Once an event is noticed, an onlooker must decide if it is truly an emergency. Emergencies are not always clearly labeled as such; "smoke" pouring into a waiting room may be caused by fire, or it may merely indicate a leak in a steam pipe. Screams in the street may signal an assault or a family quarrel. A man lying in a doorway may be having a coronary—or he may simply be sleeping off a drunk.

A person trying to interpret a situation often looks at those around him to see how he should react. If everyone else is calm and indifferent, he will tend to remain so; if everyone else is reacting strongly, he is likely to become aroused. This tendency is not merely slavish conformity; ordinarily we derive much valuable information about new situations from how others around us behave. It's a rare traveler who, in picking a roadside restaurant, chooses to stop at one where no other cars appear in the parking lot.

But occasionally the reactions of others provide false information. The studied nonchalance of patients in a dentist's waiting room is a poor indication of their inner anxiety. It is considered embarrassing to "lose your cool" in public. In a potentially acute situation, then, everyone present will appear more unconcerned that he is in fact. A crowd can thus force inaction on its members by implying, through its passivity, that an event is not an emergency. Any individual in such a crowd fears that he may appear a fool if he behaves as though it were.

To determine how the presence of other people affects a person's interpretation of an emergency, Latané and Judith Rodin set up another experiment. Subjects were paid $2 to participate in a survey of game and puzzle preferences conducted at Columbia University by the Consumer Testing Bureau. An attractive young market researcher met them at the door and took them to the testing room, where they were given questionnaires to fill out. Before leaving, she told them that she would be working next door in her office, which was separated from the room by a folding room-divider. She then entered her office, where she shuffled papers, opened drawers and made enough noise to remind the subjects of her presence. After four minutes she turned on a high-fidelity tape recorder.

On it, the subjects heard the researcher climb up on a chair, perhaps to reach for a stack of papers on the bookcase. They heard a loud crash and a scream as the chair collapsed and she fell, and they heard her moan, "Oh, my foot . . . I . . . I . . . can't move it Oh, I . . . can't get this . . . thing off me." Her cries gradually got more subdued and controlled.

Twenty-six people were alone in the waiting room when the "accident" occurred. Seventy percent of them offered to help the victim. Many pushed back the divider to offer their assistance; others called out to offer their help.

Among those waiting in pairs, only 20 percent—8 out of 40—offered to help. The other 32 remained unresponsive. In defining the situation as a nonemergency, they explained to themselves why the other member of the pair did not leave the room; they also removed any reason for action themselves. Whatever had happened, it was believed to be not serious. "A mild sprain," some said. "I didn't want to embarrass her." In a "real" emergency, they assured us, they would be among the first to help.

The Lonely Crowd

20 Even if a person defines an event as an emergency, the presence of other bystanders may still make him less likely to intervene. He feels that his responsibility is diffused and diluted. Thus, if your car breaks down on a busy highway, hundreds of drivers whiz by without anyone's stopping to help—but if you are stuck on a nearly deserted country road, whoever passes you first is likely to stop.

To test this diffusion-of-responsibility theory, we simulated an emergency in which people overheard a victim calling for help. Some thought they were the only person to hear the cries; the rest believed that others heard them, too. As with the witnesses to Kitty Genovese's murder, the subjects could not *see* one another or know what others were doing. The kind of direct group inhibition found in the other two studies could not operate.

For the simulation, we recruited 72 students at New York University to participate in what was referred to as a "group discussion" of personal problems in an urban university. Each student was put in an individual room equipped with a set of headphones and a microphone. It was explained that this precaution had been taken because participants might feel embarrassed about discussing their problems publicly. Also, the experimenter said that he would not listen to the initial discussion, but would only ask for reactions later. Each person was to talk in turn.

The first to talk reported that he found it difficult to adjust to New York and his studies. Then, hesitantly and with obvious embarrassment, he mentioned that he was prone to nervous seizures when he was under stress. Other students then talked about their own problems in turn. The number of people in the "discussion" varied. But whatever the apparent size of the group—two, three or six people—only the subject was actually present; the others, as well as the instructions and the speeches of the victim-to-be, were present only on a prerecorded tape.

When it was the first person's turn to talk again, he launched into the following performance, becoming louder and having increasing speech difficulties: "I can see a lot of er of er how other people's problems are similar to mine because er I mean er they're not er e-easy to handle sometimes and er I er um I think I I need er if if could er er somebody er er er give me give me a little er give me a little help here because er I er *uh* I've got a a one of the er seiz-er er things coming *on* and and er uh uh (choking sounds) . . ."

25   Eighty-five percent of the people who believed themselves to be 25 alone with the victim came out of their room to help. Sixty-two percent of the people who believed there was *one* other bystander did so. Of those who believed there were four other bystanders, only 31 percent reported the fit. The responsibility-diluting effect of other people was so strong that single individuals were more than twice as likely to report the emergency as those who thought other people also knew about it.

The Lesson Learned

People who failed to report the emergency showed few signs of the apathy and indifference thought to characterize "unresponsive bystanders." When the experimenter entered the room to end the situation, the subject often asked if the victim was "all right." Many of them showed physical signs of nervousness; they often had trembling hands and sweating palms. If anything, they seemed more emotionally aroused than did those who reported the emergency. Their emotional behavior was a sign of their continuing conflict concerning whether to respond or not.

Thus, the stereotype of the unconcerned, depersonalized *homo urbanus,* blandly watching the misfortunes of others, proves inaccurate. Instead, we find that a bystander to an emergency is an anguished individual in genuine doubt, wanting to do the right thing but compelled to make complex decisions under pressure of stress and fear. His reactions are shaped by the actions of others—all too frequently by their inaction.

And we are that bystander. Caught up by the apparent indifference of others, we may pass by an emergency without helping or even realizing that help is needed. Once we are aware of the influence of those around us, however, we can resist it. We can choose to see distress and step forward to relieve it.

Questions on Meaning

1. Americans tend to be distant and polite in public. Why does this distancing cause problems when there is a crisis?
2. If other people are around, everyone tends to watch others to see what to do. It takes much longer for a crowd to notice smoke and move than it does for one person. How does this "herd mentality" affect our ability to help one another?
3. People are not indifferent to one another, but even when people are upset, they might not act. How do other circumstances keep people from acting?

Questions on Rhetorical Strategy and Style

1. The essay begins with terrible incidents of people being harmed or becoming ill and not being helped. Why does this beginning draw the reader into the essay?
2. When given scientific research, a reader is more likely to believe the material in an essay. How is research used in this essay to emphasize the message?
3. This essay shows what causes human inaction and what the effects can be. How does the cause-and-effect argument help the reader to see the point of the essay?

Writing Assignments

1. Look up the cases described in the introduction to this essay, or find similar reports in current news articles. Then write about how the circumstances of the event reflect the scientific research in this essay.
2. Describe a time when you were influenced by the crowd. Why did you hesitate to act? What made you wait for someone to do something? Discuss the effects of group influence.
3. What circumstances might keep us from helping out someone who is in trouble? Why might we hesitate to stop on the road to help a stranded driver? Why do we avoid people who seem to be poor or sick, perhaps street people? What do we fear?

Lifeboat Ethics: The Case against Helping the Poor

Garrett Hardin

Garrett Hardin (1915–), a human ecology writer and philosopher, attended the University of Chicago (Sc.B, 1936) and Stanford University (Ph.D., 1941) and taught at the University of California at Santa Barbara. Hardin's books include Filters Against Folly: How to Survive Despite Economists, Ecologists, and the Merely Eloquent *(1985) and* Living within Limits: How Global Population Growth Threatens Widespread Social Disorder *(1992). In this essay, published in* Psychology Today *in 1974, Hardin argues that the distribution of food in the world is a moral issue affecting the rights of both the needy and the wealthy.*

1   Environmentalists use the metaphor of the earth as a "spaceship" in trying to persuade countries, industries and people to stop wasting and polluting our natural resources. Since we all share life on this planet, they argue, no single person or institution has the right to destroy, waste, or use more than a fair share of its resources.

But does everyone on earth have an equal right to an equal share of its resources? The spaceship metaphor can be dangerous when used by misguided idealists to justify suicidal policies for sharing our resources through uncontrolled immigration and foreign aid. In their enthusiastic but unrealistic generosity, they confuse the ethics of a spaceship with those of a lifeboat.

A true spaceship would have to be under the control of a captain, since no ship could possibly survive if its course were determined by committee. Spaceship Earth certainly has no captain; the United

Nations is merely a toothless tiger, with little power to enforce any policy upon its bickering members.

If we divide the world crudely into rich nations and poor nations, two thirds of them are desperately poor, and only one third comparatively rich, with the United States the wealthiest of all. Metaphorically each nation can be seen as a lifeboat full of comparatively rich people. In the ocean outside each lifeboat swim the poor of the world, who would like to get in, or at least to share some of the wealth. What should the lifeboat passengers do?

5   First, we must recognize the limited capacity of any lifeboat. For   5
example, a nation's land has a limited capacity to support a population and as the current energy crisis has shown us, in some ways we have already exceeded the carrying capacity of our land.

So here we sit, say fifty people in our lifeboat. To be generous let us assume it has room for ten more, making a total capacity of sixty. Suppose the fifty of us in the lifeboat see 100 others swimming in the water outside, begging for admission to our boat or for handouts. We have several options: we may be tempted to try to live by the Christian ideal of being "our brother's keeper," or by the Marxist ideal of "to each according to his needs." Since the needs of all in the water are the same, and since they can all be seen as "our brothers," we could take them all into our boat, making a total of 150 in a boat designed for sixty. The boat swamps, everyone drowns. Complete justice, complete catastrophe.

Since the boat has an unused excess capacity of ten more passengers, we could admit just ten more to it. But which ten do we let in? How do we choose? Do we pick the best ten, the neediest ten, "first come, first served"? And what do we say to the ninety we exclude? If we do let an extra ten into our lifeboat, we will have lost our "safety factor," an engineering principle of critical importance. For example, if we don't leave room for excess capacity as a safety factor in our country's agriculture, a new plant disease or a bad change in the weather could have disastrous consequences.

Suppose we decide to preserve our small safety factor and admit no more to the lifeboat. Our survival is then possible although we shall have to be constantly on guard against boarding parties.

While this last solution clearly offers the only means of our survival, it is morally abhorrent to many people. Some say they feel guilty about their good luck. My reply is simple: "Get out and yield your place to others." This may solve the problem of the guilt-ridden person's conscience, but it does not change the ethics of the lifeboat. The needy person to whom the guilt-ridden person yields his place will not himself feel guilty about his good luck. If he did, he would not climb aboard. The net result of conscience-stricken people giving up their unjustly held seats is the elimination of that sort of conscience from the lifeboat.

10   This is the basic metaphor within which we must work out our   10
solutions. Let us now enrich the image, step by step, with substantive additions from the real world, a world that must solve real and pressing problems of overpopulation and hunger.

The harsh ethics of the lifeboat become even harsher when we consider the reproductive differences between the rich nations and the poor nations. The people inside the lifeboats are doubling in numbers every eighty-seven years: those swimming around outside are doubling on the average, every thirty-five years, more than twice as fast as the rich. And since the world's resources are dwindling, the difference in prosperity between the rich and the poor can only increase.

As of 1973, the U.S. had a population of 210 million people, who were increasing by 0.8 percent per year. Outside our lifeboat, let us imagine another 210 million people (say the combined populations of Colombia, Ecuador, Venezuela, Morocco, Pakistan, Thailand and the Philippines), who are increasing at a rate of 3.3 percent per year. Put differently, the doubling time for this aggregate population is twenty-one years, compared to eighty-seven years for the U.S.

Now suppose the U.S. agreed to pool its resources with those seven countries, with everyone receiving an equal share. Initially the ratio of Americans to non-Americans in this model would be one-to-one but consider what the ratio would be after eighty-seven years, by which time the Americans would have doubled to a population of 420 million. By then, doubling every twenty-one years, the other group would have swollen to 354 billion. Each American would have to share the available resources with more than eight people.

But, one could argue, this discussion assumes that current population trends will continue, and they may not. Quite so. Most likely the rate of population increase will decline much faster in the U.S. than it will in the other countries, and there does not seem to be much we can do about it. In sharing with "each according to his needs," we must recognize that needs are determined by population size, which is determined by the rate of reproduction, which at present is regarded as a sovereign right of every nation, poor or not. This being so, the philanthropic load created by the sharing ethic of the spaceship can only increase.

15   The fundamental error of spaceship ethics, and the sharing it re-   15
quires, is that it leads to what I call "the tragedy of the commons." Under a system of private property, the men who own property recognize their responsibility to care for it, for if they don't they will eventually suffer. A farmer, for instance, will allow no more cattle in a pasture than its carrying capacity justifies. If he overloads it, erosion sets in, weeds take over, and he loses the use of the pasture.

If a pasture becomes a commons open to all, the right of each to use it may not be matched by a corresponding responsibility to protect it. Asking everyone to use it with discretion will hardly do, for the considerate herdsman who refrains from overloading the commons suffers more than a selfish one who says his needs are greater. If everyone would restrain himself all would be well; but it takes only one less than everyone to ruin a system of voluntary restraint. In a crowded world of less than perfect human beings, mutual ruin is inevitable if there are no controls. This is the tragedy of the commons.

One of the major tasks of education today should be the creation of such an acute awareness of the dangers of the commons that people will recognize its many varieties. For example, the air and water have become polluted because they are treated as commons. Further growth in the population or per-capita conversion of natural resources into pollutants will only make the problem worse. The same holds true for the fish of the oceans. Fishing fleets have nearly disappeared in many parts of the world, technological improvements in the art of fishing are hastening the day of complete ruin. Only the replacement of the system of the commons with a responsible system of control will save the land, air, water and oceanic fisheries.

In recent years there has been a push to create a new commons called a World Food Bank, an international depository of food reserves to which nations would contribute according to their abilities and from which they would draw according to their needs. This humanitarian proposal has received support from many liberal international groups, and from such prominent citizens as Margaret Mead, U.N. Secretary General Kurt Waldheim, and Senators Edward Kennedy and George McGovern.

A world food bank appeals powerfully to our humanitarian impulses. But before we rush ahead with such a plan, let us recognize where the greatest political push comes from, lest we be disillusioned later. Our experience with the "Food for Peace program," or Public Law 480, gives us the answer. This program moved billions of dollars' worth of U.S. surplus grain to food-short, population-long countries during the past two decades. But when P.L. 480 first became law, a headline in the business magazine *Forbes* revealed the real power behind it: "Feeding the World's Hungry Millions: How It Will Mean Billions for U.S. Business."

20   And indeed it did. In the years 1960 to 1970, U.S. taxpayers spent   20
a total of $7.9 billion on the Food for Peace program. Between 1948 and 1970, they also paid an additional $50 billion for other economic-aid programs, some of which went for food and food-producing machinery and technology. Though all U.S. taxpayers were forced to contribute to the cost of P.L. 480, certain special interest groups gained handsomely under the program. Farmers did not have to contribute the grain; the Government, or rather the taxpayers, bought it from them at full market prices. The increased demand raised prices of farm products generally. The manufacturers of farm machinery, fertilizers and pesticides benefited by the farmers' extra efforts to grow more food. Grain elevators profited from storing the surplus until it could be shipped. Railroads made money hauling it to ports, and shipping lines profited from carrying it overseas. The implementation of P.L. 480 required the creation of a vast Government bureaucracy, which then acquired its own vested interest in continuing the program regardless of its merits.

Those who proposed and defended the Food for Peace program in public rarely mentioned its importance to any of these special interests. The public emphasis was always on its humanitarian effects. The combination of silent selfish interests and highly vocal humanitarian apologists made a powerful and successful lobby for extracting money from taxpayers. We can expect the same lobby to push now for the creation of a World Food Bank.

However great the potential benefit to selfish interests, it should not be a decisive argument against a truly humanitarian program. We must ask if such a program would actually do more good than harm, not only momentarily but also in the long run. Those who propose the food bank usually refer to a current "emergency" or "crisis" in terms of world food supply. But what is an emergency? Although they may be infrequent and sudden, everyone knows that emergencies will occur from time to time. A well-run family, company, organization or country prepares for the likelihood of accidents and emergencies. It expects them, it budgets for them, it saves for them.

What happens if some organizations or countries budget for accidents and others do not? If each country is solely responsible for its own well-being, poorly managed ones will suffer. But they can learn from experience. They may mend their ways, and learn to budget for infrequent but certain emergencies. For example, the weather varies from year to year, and periodic crop failures are certain. A wise and competent government saves out of the production of the good years in anticipation of bad years to come. Joseph taught this policy to Pharoah in Egypt more than 2,000 years ago. Yet the great majority of the governments in the world today do not follow such a policy. They lack either the wisdom or the competence, or both. Should those nations that do manage to put something aside be forced to come to the rescue each time an emergency occurs among the poor nations?

"But it isn't their fault!" Some kind-hearted liberals argue, "How can we blame the poor people who are caught in an emergency? Why must they suffer for the sins of their governments?" The concept of blame is simply not relevant here. The real question is, what are the operational consequences of establishing a world food bank? If it is open to every country every time a need develops, slovenly rulers will not be motivated to take Joseph's advice. Someone will always come to their aid. Some countries will deposit food in the world food bank, and others will withdraw it. There will be almost no overlap. As a result of such solutions to food shortage emergencies, the poor countries will not learn to mend their ways, and will suffer progressively greater emergencies as their populations grow.

25   On the average, poor countries undergo a 2.5 percent increase in population each year; rich countries, about 0.8 percent. Only rich countries have anything in the way of food reserves set aside, and even they do not have as much as they should. Poor countries have none. If poor countries received no food from the outside, the rate of their population growth would be periodically checked by crop failures and famines. But if they can always draw on a world food bank in time of need, their population can continue to grow unchecked, and so will their "need" for aid. In the short run, a world food bank may

diminish that need, but in the long run it actually increases the need without limit.

Without some system of worldwide food sharing, the proportion of people in the rich and poor nations might eventually stabilize. The overpopulated poor countries would decrease in numbers, while the rich countries that had room for more people would increase. But with a well-meaning system of sharing, such as a world food bank, the growth differential between the rich and the poor countries will not only persist, it will increase. Because of the higher rate of population growth in the poor countries of the world, 88 percent of today's children are born poor, and only 12 percent rich. Year by year the ratio becomes worse, as the fast-reproducing poor outnumber the slow-reproducing rich.

A world food bank is thus a commons in disguise. People will have more motivation to draw from it than to add to any common store. The less provident and less able will multiply at the expense of the abler and more provident, bringing eventual ruin upon all who share in the commons. Besides, any system of "sharing" that amounts to foreign aid from the rich nations to the poor nations will carry the taint of charity, which will contribute little to the world peace so devoutly desired by those who support the idea of a world food bank.

As past U.S. foreign-aid programs have amply and depressingly demonstrated, international charity frequently inspires mistrust and antagonism rather than gratitude on the part of the recipient nation.

The modern approach to foreign aid stresses the export of technology and advice, rather than money and food. As an ancient Chinese proverb goes: "Give a man a fish and he will eat for a day; teach him how to fish and he will eat for the rest of his days." Acting on this advice, the Rockefeller and Ford Foundations have financed a number of programs for improving agriculture in the hungry nations. Known as the "Green Revolution," these programs have led to the development of "miracle rice" and "miracle wheat," new strains that offer bigger harvests and greater resistance to crop damage. Norman Borlaug, the Nobel Prize winning agronomist who, supported by the Rockefeller Foundation, developed "miracle wheat," is one of the most prominent advocates of a world food bank.

30   Whether or not the Green Revolution can increase food pro-   30 duction as much as its champions claim is a debatable but possibly irrelevant point. Those who support this well-intended humanitarian effort should first consider some of the fundamentals of human

ecology. Ironically, one man who did was the late Alan Gregg, a vice president of the Rockefeller Foundation. Two decades ago he expressed strong doubts about the wisdom of such attempts to increase food production. He likened the growth and spread of humanity over the surface of the earth to the spread of cancer in the human body, remarking that "cancerous growths demand food, but, as far as I know, they have never been cured by getting it."

Every human born constitutes a draft on all aspects of the environment: food, air, water, forests, beaches, wildlife, scenery and solitude. Food can, perhaps, be significantly increased to meet a growing demand. But what about clean beaches, unspoiled forests, and solitude? If we satisfy a growing population's need for food, we necessarily decrease its per capita supply of the other resources needed by men.

India, for example, now has a population of 600 million, which increases by 15 million each year. This population already puts a huge load on a relatively impoverished environment. The country's forests are now only a small fraction of what they were three centuries ago, and floods and erosion continually destroy the insufficient farmland that remains. Every one of the 15 million new lives added to India's population puts an additional burden on the environment, and increases the economic and social costs of crowding. However humanitarian our intent, every Indian life saved through medical or nutritional assistance from abroad diminishes the quality of life for those who remain, and for subsequent generations. If rich countries make it possible, through foreign aid, for 600 million Indians to swell to 1.2 billion in a mere 28 years, as their current growth rate threatens, will future generations of Indians thank us for hastening the destruction of their environment? Will our good intentions be sufficient excuse for the consequences of our actions?

My final example of a commons in action is one for which the public has the least desire for rational discussion—immigration. Anyone who publicly questions the wisdom of current U.S. immigration policy is promptly charged with bigotry, prejudice, ethnocentrism, chauvinism, isolationism or selfishness. Rather than encounter such accusations, one would rather talk about other matters, leaving immigration policy to wallow in the crosscurrents of special interests that take no account of the good of the whole, or the interests of posterity.

Perhaps we still feel guilty about things we said in the past. Two generations ago the popular press frequently referred to Dagos, Wops,

Polacks, Chinks and Krauts, in articles about how America was being "overrun" by foreigners of supposedly inferior genetic stock. But because the implied inferiority of foreigners was used then as justification for keeping them out, people now assume that restrictive policies could only be based on such misguided notions. There are other grounds.

35   Just consider the numbers involved. Our Government acknowl- 35
edges a net inflow of 400,000 immigrants a year. While we have no hard data on the extent of illegal entries, educated guesses put the figure at about 600,000 a year. Since the natural increase (excess of births over deaths) of the resident population now runs about 1.7 million per year, the yearly gain from immigration amounts to at least 19 percent of the total annual increase, and may be as much as 37 percent if we include the estimate for illegal immigrants. Considering the growing use of birth-control devices, the potential effect of educational campaigns by such organizations as Planned Parenthood Federation of America and Zero Population Growth, and the influence of inflation and the housing shortage, the fertility rate of American women may decline so much that immigration could account for all the yearly increase in population. Should we not at least ask if that is what we want?

For the sake of those who worry about whether the "quality" of the average immigrant compares favorably with the quality of the average resident, let us assume that immigrants and nativeborn citizens are of exactly equal quality, however one defines that term. We will focus here only on quantity; and since our conclusions will depend on nothing else, all charges of bigotry and chauvinism become irrelevant.

World food banks *move food to the people*, hastening the exhaustion of the environment of the poor countries. Unrestricted immigration, on the other hand, *moves people to the food*, thus speeding up the destruction of the environment of the rich countries. We can easily understand why poor people should want to make this latter transfer, but why should rich hosts encourage it?

As is the case of foreign-aid programs, immigration receives support from selfish interests and humanitarian impulses. The primary selfish interest in unimpeded immigration is the desire of employers for cheap labor, particularly in industries and trades that offer degrading work. In the past, one wave of foreigners after another was brought into the U.S. to work at wretched jobs for wretched wages.

In recent years the Cubans, Puerto Ricans and Mexicans have had this dubious honor. The interests of the employers of cheap labor mesh well with the guilty silence of the country's liberal intelligentsia. White Anglo-Saxon Protestants are particularly reluctant to call for a closing of the doors to immigration for fear of being called bigots.

But not all countries have such reluctant leadership. Most educated Hawaiians, for example, are keenly aware of the limits of their environment, particularly in terms of population growth. There is only so much room on the islands, and the islanders know it. To Hawaiians, immigrants from the other 49 states present as great a threat as those from other nations. At a recent meeting of Hawaiian government officials in Honolulu, I had the ironic delight of hearing a speaker, who like most of his audience was of Japanese ancestry, ask how the country might practically and constitutionally close its door to further immigration. One member of the audience countered: "How can we shut the doors now? We have many friends and relatives in Japan that we'd like to bring here some day so that they can enjoy Hawaii too." The Japanese-American speaker smiled sympathetically and answered: "Yes, but we have children now, and someday we'll have grandchildren too. We can bring more people here from Japan only by giving away some of the land that we hope to pass on to our grandchildren some day. What right do we have to do that?"

At this point, I can hear U.S. liberals asking: "How can you justify slamming the door once you're inside? You say that immigrants should be kept out. But aren't we all immigrants, or the descendants of immigrants? If we insist on staying, must we not admit all others?" Our craving for intellectual order leads us to seek and prefer symmetrical rules and morals: a single rule for me and everybody else; the same rule yesterday, today and tomorrow. Justice, we feel, should not change with time and place.

We Americans of non-Indian ancestry can look upon ourselves as the descendants of thieves who are guilty morally, if not legally, of stealing this land from its Indian owners. Should we then give back the land to the now living American descendants of those Indians? However morally or logically sound this proposal may be, I, for one, am unwilling to live by it and I know no one else who is. Besides, the logical consequence would be absurd. Suppose that, intoxicated with a sense of pure justice, we should decide to turn our land over to the Indians. Since all our other wealth has also been derived from the land, wouldn't we be morally obliged to give that back to the Indians too?

Clearly, the concept of pure justice produces an infinite regression to absurdity. Centuries ago, wise men invented statutes of limitations to justify the rejection of such pure justice, in the interest of preventing continual disorder. The law zealously defends property rights, but only relatively recent property rights. Drawing a line after an arbitrary time has elapsed may be unjust, but the alternatives are worse.

We are all the descendants of thieves, and the world's resources are inequitably distributed. But we must begin the journey to tomorrow from the point where we are today. We cannot remake the past. We cannot safely divide the wealth equitably among all peoples so long as people reproduce at different rates. To do so would guarantee that our grandchildren, and everyone else's grandchildren, would have only a ruined world to inhabit.

To be generous with one's own possessions is quite different from being generous with those of posterity. We should call this point to the attention of those who, from a commendable love of justice and equality, would institute a system of the commons, either in the form of a world food bank, or of unrestricted immigration. We must convince them if we wish to save at least some parts of the world from environmental ruin.

Without a true world government to control reproduction and the use of available resources, the sharing ethic of the spaceship is impossible. For the foreseeable future, our survival demands that we govern our actions by the ethics of a lifeboat, harsh though they may be. Posterity will be satisfied with nothing less.

Questions on Meaning

1. What is Hardin's thesis? What relevance does his argument have today, as opposed to in 1974 when this essay was written?
2. Why does Hardin choose the "lifeboat" metaphor for the earth? Why does he feel the "spaceship" metaphor is faulty?
3. Explain the "tragedy of the commons." What examples does he give for "commons"?

Questions on Rhetorical Strategy and Style

1. How does Hardin compare and contrast the "World Food Bank" to the "Food for Peace" program? Why does he disagree with these efforts by rich nations to help poor nations? Explain why you concur or disagree with his position.
2. How does Hardin's discussion of Hawaii buttress his support of immigration policies?
3. In this essay, Hardin predicts that "U.S. liberals" will reject his beliefs by saying that "justice should not change with time and place." How convincing are his arguments against those who would disagree with him? Does his privileged background (Ivy League education, employment in Santa Barbara where many movie stars live) impair his credibility?

Writing Assignments

1. Checking population growth in poor countries by allowing crop failure and famine to take their toll, as Hardin proposes, is another way of suggesting that rich nations stand by while residents of poor nations starve. How do you react to that approach to population growth and world hunger? What alternatives would you suggest that might save lives and provide for the future?
2. Explore the current immigration policies of the United States. What are the arguments for and against tightening immigration requirements? Who are the major proponents and opponents of stricter immigration laws?
3. Research the idea of "sustainability" and write an essay about application of those theories in the United States today. Describe where we are approaching sustainability and where we need to address wasteful practices.

American Ignorance of War
Czeslaw Milosz

*Czeslaw Milosz (1911–) was born in Lithuania, under
Czarist Russia's control, and was living in Poland when
Germany invaded and occupied that country in 1939. In
1946, he became a diplomat for Poland's Communist government, until 1951 when he defected to the West and
eventually settled in the United States. He began writing
poetry when still a university student in Lithuania and became what many critics have called Poland's greatest modern poet, although his works were not published in that
country before 1980. In America, he became a professor at
the University of California at Berkeley and continued
writing poetry, fiction, and nonfiction. His key books include over a dozen books of poetry, two novels and the nonfiction books* The Captive Mind *(1953), from which the
following selection comes;* Native Realm *(1983); and* The
History of Polish Literature *(1983). In 1980 Milosz received the Nobel Prize for Literature. The excerpt following was published soon after Milosz came to the United
States, and in it he explains to Americans a great difference
between our perceptions of the world and what he has ex-
perienced under totalitarian regimes.*

1   "Are Americans *really* stupid?" I was asked in Warsaw. In the   1
voice of the man who posed the question, there was despair,
as well as the hope that I would contradict him. This question reveals the attitude of the average person in the people's democra-
cies toward the West: it is despair mixed with a residue of hope.

During the last few years, the West has given these people a number of reasons to despair politically. In the case of the intellectual, other, more complicated reasons come into play. Before the countries of Central and Eastern Europe entered the sphere of the Imperium, they lived through the Second World War. That war was much more devastating there than in the countries of Western Europe. It destroyed not only their economies, but also a great many values which had seemed till then unshakable.

Man tends to regard the order he lives in as *natural.* The houses he passes on his way to work seem more like rocks rising out of the earth than like products of human hands. He considers the work he does in his office or factory as essential to the harmonious functioning of the world. The clothes he wears are exactly what they should be, and he laughs at the idea that he might equally well be wearing a Roman toga or medieval armor. He respects and envies a minister of state or a bank director, and regards the possession of a considerable amount of money as the main guarantee of peace and security. He cannot believe that one day a rider may appear on a street he knows well, where cats sleep and children play, and start catching passersby with his lasso. He is accustomed to satisfying those of his physiological needs which are considered private as discreetly as possible, without realizing that such a pattern of behavior is not common to all human societies. In a word, he behaves a little like Charlie Chaplin in *The Gold Rush,* bustling about in a shack poised precariously on the edge of a cliff.

His first stroll along a street littered with glass from bomb-shattered windows shakes his faith in the "naturalness" of his world. The wind scatters papers from hastily evacuated offices, papers labeled "Confidential" or "Top Secret" that evoke visions of safes, keys, conferences, couriers, and secretaries. Now the wind blows them through the street for anyone to read; yet no one does, for each man is more urgently concerned with finding a loaf of bread. Strangely enough, the world goes on even though the offices and secret files have lost all meaning. Farther down the street, he stops before a house split in half by a bomb, the privacy of people's homes—the family smells, the warmth of the beehive life, the furniture preserving the memory of loves and hatreds—cut open to public view. The house itself, no longer a rock, but a scaffolding of plaster, concrete, and brick; and on the third floor, a solitary white bathtub, rain-rinsed of all recollection of those who once bathed in it. Its formerly influential and respected owners, now destitute, walk the fields in search of stray potatoes. Thus overnight money loses its value and becomes a meaningless mass of printed paper. His walk takes him past a little boy poking a stick into a heap of smoking ruins and whistling a song about the great leader who will preserve the nation against all enemies. The song remains, but the leader of yesterday is already part of an extinct past.

He finds he acquires new habits quickly. Once, had he stumbled upon a corpse on the street, he would have called the police. A crowd would have gathered, and much talk and comment would have ensued. Now he knows he must avoid the dark body lying in the gutter, and refrain from asking unnecessary questions. The man who fired the gun must have had his reasons; he might well have been executing an Underground sentence.

Nor is the average European accustomed to thinking of his native city as divided into segregated living areas, but a single decree can force him to this new pattern of life and thought. Quarter A may suddenly be designated for one race; B, for a second; C, for a third. As the resettlement deadline approaches, the streets become filled with long lines of wagons, carts, wheelbarrows, and people carrying bundles, beds, chests, caldrons, and bird cages. When all the moves are effected, 2,000 people may find themselves in a building that once housed 200, but each man is at last in the proper area. Then high walls are erected around quarter C, and daily a given lot of men, women, and children are loaded into wagons that take them off to specially constructed factories where they are scientifically slaughtered and their bodies burned.

And even the rider with the lasso appears, in the form of a military van waiting at the corner of a street. A man passing that corner meets a leveled rifle, raises his hands, is pushed into the van, and from that moment is lost to his family and friends. He may be sent to a concentration camp, or he may face a firing squad, his lips sealed with plaster lest he cry out against the state; but, in any case, he serves as a warning to his fellow men. Perhaps one might escape such a fate by remaining at home. But the father of a family must go out in order to provide bread and soup for his wife and children; and every night they worry about whether or not he will return. Since these conditions last for years, everyone gradually comes to look upon the city as a jungle, and upon the fate of twentieth-century man as identical with that of a caveman living in the midst of powerful monsters.

It was once thought obvious that a man bears the same name and surname throughout his entire life; now it proves wiser for many reasons to change them and to memorize a new and fabricated biography. As a result, the records of the civilian state become completely confused. Everyone ceases to care about formalities, so that marriage, for example, comes to mean little more than living together.

Respectable citizens used to regard banditry as a crime. Today, bank robbers are heroes because the money they steal is destined for the Underground. Usually they are young boys, mothers' boys, but their appearance is deceiving. The killing of a man presents no great moral problem to them.

10   The nearness of death destroys shame. Men and women change   10 as soon as they know that the date of their execution has been fixed by a fat little man with shiny boots and a riding crop. They copulate in public, on the small bit of ground surrounded by barbed wire— their last home on earth. Boys and girls in their teens, about to go off to the barricades to fight against tanks with pistols and bottles of gasoline, want to enjoy their youth and lose their respect for standards of decency.

Which world is "natural"? That which existed before, or the world of war? Both are natural, if both are within the realm of one's experience. All the concepts men live by are a product of the historic formation in which they find themselves. Fluidity and constant change are the characteristics of phenomena. And man is so plastic a being that one can even conceive of the day when a thoroughly self-respecting citizen will crawl on all fours, sporting a tail of brightly colored feathers as a sign of conformity to the order he lives in.

The man of the East cannot take Americans seriously because they have never undergone the experiences that teach men how relative their judgements and thinking habits are. Their resultant lack of imagination is appalling. Because they were born and raised in a given social order and in a given system of values, they believe that any other order must be "unnatural," and that it cannot last because it is incompatible with human nature. But even they may one day know fire, hunger, and the sword. In all probability this is what will occur; for it is hard to believe that when one half of the world is living through terrible disasters, the other half can continue a nineteenth-century mode of life, learning about the distress of its distant fellow men only from movies and newspapers. Recent examples teach us that this cannot be. An inhabitant of Warsaw or Budapest once looked at newsreels of bombed Spain or burning Shanghai, but in the end he learned how these and many other catastrophes appear in actuality. He read a gloomy tale of the NKVD until one day he found he himself had to deal with it. *If something exists in one place, it will exist everywhere.* This is the conclusion he draws from his observations, and so he has no particular faith in the momentary prosperity of America. He suspects that the years 1933–1945 in Europe prefigure what will occur elsewhere. A hard school, where ignorance was punished not by bad marks but by death, has taught him to think sociologically and historically. But it has not freed him from irrational feelings. He is apt to believe in theories that foresee violent changes in the countries of the West, for he finds it unjust that they should escape the hardships he had to undergo.

Questions on Meaning

1. What does Milosz mean by "the natural world"?
2. Why is it that Eastern Europeans "cannot take Americans seriously"? How seriously can Americans take themselves in this respect?
3. Fully explain the meaning of Milosz's statement: "If something exists in one place, it will exist everywhere."

Questions on Rhetorical Strategy and Style

1. The essay uses examples to show us what life is like under a totalitarian government. Reread that section of the essay and identify three specific descriptions that you find vivid, and explain how the language used creates this effect.
2. Milosz describes the Nazi occupation of Poland without referring to Nazis or historical specifics. In this section of the essay, from paragraph 4 through 10, he uses the present tense to describe these changed conditions. What are the effects on the reader of his decisions to write the essay in this way? What would be lost if it had been written as conventional history in past tense with names, places, and dates?

Writing Assignments

1. Milosz's statement that the peaceful democratic world in which Americans live is no more natural than the uncertain, violent world of authoritarian and military rule is somewhat shocking to many readers. How did you react as you read this? What is the difference between *knowing about* a horrible experience such as Milosz describes, or the fact of 6 million Jews put to death in Nazi death camps, and actually *experiencing or observing* it firsthand?
2. The title of this 1953 essay implies Americans are ignorant of war, but the essay actually means Americans are ignorant of the effects of being occupied by an opposing force during wartime. How ignorant are Americans of war itself, particularly after the extensive television coverage of our last two wars: the Vietnam War and the Gulf War? Neither was fought on American soil, of course, but in both the death of American soldiers was well publicized. Write an essay in which you describe how the country as a whole views war.

3. This essay, like almost any reading in world history, is a blunt reminder that human beings are capable of great atrocities and violence. What is your view of human nature? Write an essay in which you address this question. Try to define your view of human nature in a way that includes both your everyday outlook and your understanding of the darker realities.

The Perils of Indifference

Elie Wiesel

Elie Wiesel (1928–) was born in the village of Sighet in Romania to a religious Jewish family. In 1944 his life changed when his family was deported by the Nazis to Auschwitz, where his father died in 1945. After the camp was liberated by the Allied forces, Wiesel spent a few years in a French orphanage. In 1948 he entered the Sorbonne and began writing for the newspaper L'arche. *In 1954 he made the decision to write about the Holocaust, which led to the publication of his first book,* Night *(1958), followed by* Jews of Silence *(1966). In 1963 he became a U.S. citizen. In 1978 he was appointed chair of the Presidential Commission on the Holocaust, which led to the American memorial monument to the victims of Nazi oppression during World War II. In 1985 Wiesel received the Congressional Gold Medal of Achievement. The following year he received the Nobel Peace Prize. He has written numerous books dealing with the Holocaust, hatred, racism, genocide, and faith, including* Sages and Dreamers *(1991), and his memoir* All Rivers Run to the Sea *(1995). In the following speech he addresses Congress and the President about the need for vigilance in the face of evil.*

1   Mr. President, Mrs. Clinton, members of Congress, Ambassador Holbrooke, Excellencies, friends:

Fifty-four years ago to the day, a young Jewish boy from a small town in the Carpathian Mountains woke up, not far from Goethe's beloved Weimar, in a place of eternal infamy called Buchenwald. He was finally free, but there was no joy in his heart. He thought there never would be again. Liberated a day earlier by American soldiers, he remembers their rage at what they saw. And even if he lives to be a very old man, he will always be grateful to them for that rage, and also for their compassion. Though he did not understand their language, their eyes told him what he needed to know—that they, too, would remember, and bear witness.

And now, I stand before you, Mr. President—Commander-in-Chief of the army that freed me, and tens of thousands of others—and I am filled with a profound and abiding gratitude to the American people. Gratitude is a word that I cherish. Gratitude is what defines the humanity of the human being. And I am grateful to you, Hillary, or Mrs. Clinton, for what you said, and for what you are doing for children in the world, for the homeless, for the victims of injustice, the victims of destiny and society. And I thank all of you for being here.

We are on the threshold of a new century, a new millennium. What will the legacy of this vanishing century be? How will it be remembered in the new millennium? Surely it will be judged, and judged severely, in both moral and metaphysical terms. These failures have cast a dark shadow over humanity: two World Wars, countless civil wars, the senseless chain of assassinations (Gandhi, the Kennedys, Martin Luther King, Sadat, Rabin), bloodbaths in Cambodia and Nigeria, India and Pakistan, Ireland and Rwanda, Eritrea and Ethiopia, Sarajevo and Kosovo; the inhumanity in the gulag and the tragedy of Hiroshima. And, on a different level, of course, Auschwitz and Treblinka. So much violence; so much indifference.

5 What is indifference? Etymologically, the word means "no difference." A strange and unnatural state in which the lines blur between light and darkness, dusk and dawn, crime and punishment, cruelty and compassion, good and evil. What are its courses and inescapable consequences? Is it a philosophy? Is there a philosophy of indifference conceivable? Can one possibly view indifference as a virtue? Is it necessary at times to practice it simply to keep one's sanity, live normally, enjoy a fine meal and a glass of wine, as the world around us experiences harrowing upheavals?

Of course, indifference can be tempting—more than that, seductive. It is so much easier to look away from victims. It is so much easier to avoid such rude interruptions to our work, our dreams, our hopes.

It is, after all, awkward, troublesome, to be involved in another person's pain and despair. Yet, for the person who is indifferent, his or her neighbor are of no consequence. And, therefore, their lives are meaningless. Their hidden or even visible anguish is of no interest. Indifference reduces the Other to an abstraction.

Over there, behind the black gates of Auschwitz, the most tragic of all prisoners were the "Muselmanner," as they were called. Wrapped in their torn blankets, they would sit or lie on the ground, staring vacantly into space, unaware of who or where they were—strangers to their surroundings. They no longer felt pain, hunger, thirst. They feared nothing. They felt nothing. They were dead and did not know it.

Rooted in our tradition, some of us felt that to be abandoned by humanity then was not the ultimate. We felt that to be abandoned by God was worse than to be punished by Him. Better an unjust God than an indifferent one. For us to be ignored by God was a harsher punishment than to be a victim of His anger. Man can live far from God—not outside God. God is wherever we are. Even in suffering? Even in suffering.

In a way, to be indifferent to that suffering is what makes the human being inhuman. Indifference, after all, is more dangerous than anger and hatred. Anger can at times be creative. One writes a great poem, a great symphony. One does something special for the sake of humanity because one is angry at the injustice that one witnesses. But indifference is never creative. Even hatred at times may elicit a response. You fight it. You denounce it. You disarm it.

10 Indifference elicits no response. Indifference is not a response. In- 10 difference is not a beginning; it is an end. And, therefore, indifference is always the friend of the enemy, for it benefits the aggressor—never his victim, whose pain is magnified when he or she feels forgotten. The political prisoner in his cell, the hungry children, the homeless refugees—not to respond to their plight, not to relieve their solitude by offering them a spark of hope is to exile them from human memory. And in denying their humanity, we betray our own.

Indifference, then, is not only a sin, it is a punishment.

And this is one of the most important lessons of this outgoing century's wide-ranging experiments in good and evil.

In the place that I come from, society was composed of three simple categories: the killers, the victims, and the bystanders. During the darkest of times, inside the ghettoes and death camps—and I'm glad that Mrs. Clinton mentioned that we are now commemorating that event, that period, that we are now in the Days of Remembrance—but then, we felt abandoned, forgotten. All of us did.

And our only miserable consolation was that we believed that Auschwitz and Treblinka were closely guarded secrets; that the leaders of the free world did not know what was going on behind those black gates and barbed wire; that they had no knowledge of the war against the Jews that Hitler's armies and their accomplices waged as part of the war against the Allies. If they knew, we thought, surely those leaders would have moved heaven and earth to intervene. They would have spoken out with great outrage and conviction. They would have bombed the railways leading to Birkenau, just the railways, just once.

15 And now we knew, we learned, we discovered that the Pentagon 15 knew, the State Department knew. And the illustrious occupant of the White House then, who was a great leader—and I say it with some anguish and pain, because, today is exactly 54 years marking his death—Franklin Delano Roosevelt died on April the 12th, 1945. So he is very much present to me and to us. No doubt, he was a great leader. He mobilized the American people and the world, going into battle, bringing hundreds and thousands of valiant and brave soldiers in America to fight fascism, to fight dictatorship, to fight Hitler. And so many of the young people fell in battle. And, nevertheless, his image in Jewish history—I must say it—his image in Jewish history is flawed.

The depressing tale of the *St. Louis* is a case in point. Sixty years ago, its human cargo—nearly 1,000 Jews—was turned back to Nazi Germany. And that happened after the Kristallnacht, after the first state sponsored pogrom, with hundreds of Jewish shops destroyed, synagogues burned, thousands of people put in concentration camps. And that ship, which was already in the shores of the United States, was sent back. I don't understand. Roosevelt was a good man, with a heart. He understood those who needed help. Why didn't he allow these refugees to disembark? A thousand people—in America, the great country, the greatest democracy, the most generous of all new nations in modern history. What happened? I don't understand. Why the indifference, on the highest level, to the suffering of the victims?

But then, there were human beings who were sensitive to our tragedy. Those non-Jews, those Christians, that we call the "Righteous Gentiles," whose selfless acts of heroism saved the honor of their faith. Why were they so few? Why was there a greater effort to save SS murderers after the war than to save their victims during the war? Why did some of America's largest corporations continue to do business with Hitler's Germany until 1942? It has been suggested, and it was documented, that the Wehrmacht could not have conducted its invasion of France without oil obtained from American sources. How is one to explain their indifference?

And yet, my friends, good things have also happened in this traumatic century: the defeat of Nazism, the collapse of communism, the rebirth of Israel on its ancestral soil, the demise of apartheid, Israel's peace treaty with Egypt, the peace accord in Ireland. And let us remember the meeting, filled with drama and emotion, between Rabin and Arafat that you, Mr. President, convened in this very place. I was here and I will never forget it.

And then, of course, the joint decision of the United States and NATO to intervene in Kosovo and save those victims, those refugees, those who were uprooted by a man, whom I believe that because of his crimes, should be charged with crimes against humanity.

20 But this time, the world was not silent. This time, we do respond. 20 This time, we intervene.

Does it mean that we have learned from the past? Does it mean that society has changed? Has the human being become less indifferent and more human? Have we really learned from our experiences? Are we less insensitive to the plight of victims of ethnic cleansing and other forms of injustices in places near and far? Is today's justified intervention in Kosovo, led by you, Mr. President, a lasting warning that never again will the deportation, the terrorization of children and their parents, be allowed anywhere in the world? Will it discourage other dictators in other lands to do the same?

What about the children? Oh, we see them on television, we read about them in the papers, and we do so with a broken heart. Their fate is always the most tragic, inevitably. When adults wage war, children perish. We see their faces, their eyes. Do we hear their pleas? Do we feel their pain, their agony? Every minute one of them dies of disease, violence, famine.

Some of them—so many of them—could be saved.

And so, once again, I think of the young Jewish boy from the Carpathian Mountains. He has accompanied the old man I have become throughout these years of quest and struggle. And together we walk towards the new millennium, carried by profound fear and extraordinary hope.

Questions on Meaning

1. Wiesel defines indifference as a "strange and unnatural state." What is your definition? How can indifference be unnatural?

2. What does the author mean by "Better an unjust God than an indifferent one"? How does this relate to the way various theologies explanation why bad things happen to good people?

3. How aware were you that the United States knew about the concentration camps? Explain what you understand about that time in history.

Questions on Rhetorical Strategy and Style

1. How does the tone of Wiesel's speech acknowledge or account for the significance of the day? Why does he open with a personal recollection?

2. What is the rhetorical purpose of referring to the "new millennium [and] the legacy of this vanishing century"? What is the metaphoric significance of "vanishing" in this context?

3. The speech essentially offers an extended definition of indifference. Describe how that definition develops over the course of the occasion.

Writing Assignments

1. Wiesel refers to more recent examples of genocide, such as in Rwanda and Kosovo. Write an essay explaining what occurred in these places and why.

2. Toward the end of his speech, Wiesel asks whether we have learned from the past. "Has the human being become less indifferent and more human?" Write an essay in which you respond to this question. What is your answer?

The Pain of Animals

David Suzuki

*Born in Vancouver, David Suzuki (1936–) has worked
as a research scientist, environmentalist, and broadcaster
who deals with the relationships among social, economic,
and ecological needs. A professor of zoology at the University
of British Columbia until 2001, he is currently at the
Sustainable Development Research Institute (UBC). In this
essay Suzuki details the price that animals pay for human
progress.*

1   Medical technology has taken us beyond the normal barriers
of life and death and thereby created unprecedented choices
in *human* lives. Until recently, we have taken for granted our
right to use other species in any way we see fit. Food, clothing, mus-
cle power have been a few of the benefits we've derived from this
exploitation. This tradition has continued into scientific research where
animals are studied and "sacrificed" for human benefit. Now serious
questions are being asked about our right to do this.

Modern biological research is based on a shared evolutionary history of organisms that enables us to extrapolate from one organism to
another. Thus, most fundamental concepts in heredity were first shown
in fruit flies, molecular genetics began using bacteria and viruses and
much of physiology and psychology has been based on studies in mice
and rats. But today, as extinction rates have multiplied as a result of
human activity, we have begun to ask what right we have to use all
other animate forms simply to increase human knowledge or for profit
or entertainment. Underlying the "animal rights" movement is the trou-
bling question of where we fit in the rest of the natural world.

When I was young, one of my prized possessions was a BB gun.
Dad taught me how to use it safely and I spent many hours

wandering through the woods in search of prey. It's not easy to get close enough to a wild animal to kill it with a BB gun, but I did hit a few pigeons and starlings. I ate everything I shot. Then as a teenager, I graduated to a .22 rifle and with it, I killed rabbits and even shot a pheasant once.

One year I saw an ad for a metal slingshot in a comic book. I ordered it, and when it arrived, I practised for weeks shooting marbles at a target. I got to be a pretty good shot and decided to go after something live. Off I went to the woods and soon spotted a squirrel minding its own business doing whatever squirrels do. I gave chase and began peppering marbles at it until finally it jumped onto a tree, ran to the top and found itself trapped. I kept blasting away and grazed it a couple of times so it was only a matter of time before I would knock it down. Suddenly, the squirrel began to cry—a piercing shriek of terror and anguish. That animal's wail shook me to the core and I was overwhelmed with horror and shame at what I was doing—for no other reason than conceit with my prowess with a slingshot, I was going to *kill* another being. I threw away the slingshot and my guns and have never hunted again.

5   All my life, I have been an avid fisherman. Fish have always been the main source of meat protein in my family, and I have never considered fishing a sport. But there is no denying that it is exciting to reel in a struggling fish. We call it "playing" the fish, as if the wild animal's desperate struggle for survival is some kind of game.

I did "pleasure-fish" once while filming for a television report on the science of fly fishing. We fished a famous trout stream in the Catskill Mountains of New York state where all fish had to be caught and released. The fish I caught had mouths gouged and pocked by previous encounters with hooks. I found no pleasure in it because to me fish are to be caught for consumption. Today, I continue to fish for food, but I do so with a profound awareness that I am a predator of animals possessing well-developed nervous systems that detect pain. Fishing and hunting have forced me to confront the way we exploit other animals.

I studied the genetics of fruit flies for twenty-five years and during that time probably raised and killed tens of millions of them without a thought. In the early seventies, my lab discovered a series of mutations affecting behaviour of flies, and this find led us into an investigation of nerves and muscles. I applied for and received research funds to study behaviour in flies on the basis of the *similarity* of their neuromuscular systems to ours. In fact, psychologists and neurobiologists analyse behaviour, physiology and neuroanatomy of guinea pigs, rats, mice and other animals as *models* for human behaviour. So our nervous systems must closely resemble those of other mammals.

These personal anecdotes raise uncomfortable questions. What gives us the right to exploit other living organisms as we see fit? How do we know that these other creatures don't feel pain or anguish just as we do? Perhaps there's no problem with fruit flies, but where do we draw the line? I used to rationalize angling because fish are cold-blooded, as if warm-bloodedness indicates some kind of demarcation of brain development or greater sensitivity to pain. But anyone who has watched a fish's frantic fight to escape knows that it exhibits all the manifestations of pain and fear.

I've been thinking about these questions again after spending a weekend in the Queen Charlotte Islands watching grey whales close up. The majesty and freedom of these magnificent mammals contrasted strikingly with the appearance of whales imprisoned in aquariums. Currently, the Vancouver Public Aquarium is building a bigger pool for some of its whales. In a radio interview, an aquarium representative was asked whether even the biggest pool can be adequate for animals that normally have the entire ocean to rove. Part of her answer was that if we watched porpoises in the pool, we'd see that "they are quite happy."

10   That woman was projecting human perceptions and emotions   10
on the porpoises. Our ability to empathize with other people and living things is one of our endearing qualities. Just watch someone with a beloved pet, an avid gardener with plants or, for that matter, even an owner of a new car and you will see how readily we can personalize and identify with another living organism or an object. But are we justified in our inferences about captive animals in their cages?

Most wild animals have evolved with a built-in need to move freely over vast distances, fly in the air or swim through the ocean. Can a wild animal imprisoned in a small cage or pool, removed from its habitat and forced to conform to the impositions of our demands, ever be considered "happy"?

Animal rights activists are questioning our right to exploit animals, especially in scientific research. Scientists are understandably defensive, especially after labs have been broken into, experiments ruined and animals "liberated." But just as I have had to question my hunting and fishing, scientists cannot avoid confronting the issues raised, especially in relation to our closest relatives, the primates.

People love to watch monkeys in a circus or zoo and a great deal of the amusement comes from the recognition of ourselves in them. But our relationship with them is closer than just superficial similarities. When doctors at Loma Linda hospital in California implanted the heart of a baboon into the chest of Baby Fae, they were exploiting our close *biological* relationship.

Any reports on experimentation with familiar mammals like cats and dogs are sure to raise alarm among the lay public. But the use of primates is most controversial. In September 1987, at the Wildlife Film Festival in Bath, England, I watched a film shot on December 7, 1986, by a group of animal liberationists who had broken into SEMA, a biomedical research facility in Maryland. It was such a horrifying document that many in the audience rushed out after a few minutes. There were many scenes that I could not watch. As the intruders entered the facility, the camera followed to peer past cage doors, opened to reveal the animals inside. I am not ashamed to admit that I wept as baby monkeys deprived of any contact with other animals seized the fingers of their liberators and clung to them as our babies would to us. Older animals cowered in their tiny prisons, shaking from fear at the sudden appearance of people.

15   The famous chimpanzee expert, Jane Goodall, also screened the   15
same film and as a result asked for permission to visit the SEMA facility. This is what she saw (*American Scientist,* November–December 1987):

> Room after room was lined with small, bare cages, stacked one above the other, in which monkeys circled round and round and chimpanzees sat huddled, far gone in depression and despair.
>
> Young chimpanzees, three or four years old, were crammed, two together into tiny cages measuring 57 cm by 57 cm and only 61 cm high. They could hardly turn around. Not yet part of any experiment, they had been confined to these cages for more than three months.
>
> The chimps had each other for comfort, but they would not remain together for long. Once they are infected, probably with hepatitis, they will be separated and placed in another cage. And there they will remain, living in conditions of severe sensory deprivation, for the next several years. During that time they will become insane.

Goodall's horror sprang from an intimate knowledge of chimpanzees in their native habitat. There, she has learned, chimps are nothing like the captive animals that we know. In the wild, they are highly social, requiring constant interaction and physical contact. They travel long distances, and they rest in soft beds they make in the trees. Laboratory cages do not provide the conditions needed to fulfill the needs of these social, emotional and highly intelligent animals.

Ian Redmond (*BBC Wildlife*, April 1988) gives us a way to understand the horror of what lab conditions do to chimps:

> Imagine locking a two- or three-year-old child in a metal box the size of an isolette—solid walls, floor and ceiling, and a glass door that clamps shut, blotting out most external sounds—and then leaving him or her for months, the only contact, apart from feeding, being when the door swings open and masked figures reach in and take samples of blood or tissue before shoving him back and clamping the door shut again. Over the past 10 years, 94 young chimps at SEMA have endured this procedure.

Chimpanzees, along with the gorilla, are our closest relatives, sharing ninety-nine per cent of our genes. And it's that biological proximity that makes them so useful for research—we can try out experiments, study infections and test vaccines on them as models for people. And although there are only about 40,000 chimps left in the wild, compared to millions a few decades ago, the scientific demand for more has increased with the discovery of AIDS.

No chimpanzee has ever contracted AIDS, but the virus grows in them, so scientists argue that chimps will be invaluable for testing vaccines. On February 19, 1988, the National Institute of Health in the U.S. co-sponsored a meeting to discuss the use of chimpanzees in research. Dr. Maurice Hilleman, Director of the Merck Institute for Therapeutic Research, reported:

> We need more chimps. . . . The chimpanzee is certainly a threatened species and there have been bans on importing the animal into the United States and into other countries, even though . . . the chimpanzee is considered to be an agricultural pest in many parts of the world where it exists. And secondly, it's being destroyed by virtue of environmental encroachment—that is, destroying the natural habitat. So these chimpanzees are being eliminated by virtue of their being an agricultural pest and by the fact that their habitat is being

destroyed. So why not rescue them? The number of chimpanzees for AIDS research in the United States [is] somewhere in the hundreds and certainly, we need thousands.

20   Our capacity to rationalize our behaviour and needs is remarkable.   20 Chimpanzees have occupied their niche over tens of millennia of biological evolution. *We* are newcomers who have encroached on *their* territory, yet by defining them as *pests* we render them expendable. As Redmond says, "The fact that the chimpanzee is our nearest zoological relative makes it perhaps the unluckiest animal on earth, because what the kinship has come to mean is that we feel free to do most of the things to a chimp that we mercifully refrain from doing to each other."

And so the impending epidemic of AIDS confronts us not only with our inhumanity to each other but to other species.

Questions on Meaning

1. What is Suzuki's point of view on the use of animals for scientific research? Point to specific statements in the text to support your answer.
2. What useful social purpose is served by keeping whales in aquariums? What harm is done to the animals?
3. Based on the evidence Suzuki presents, what is the greatest harm that results from the use of animals for scientific purposes? Explain.

Questions on Strategy and Style

1. Why does Suzuki begin with the story of his childhood experience hunting with a BB gun?
2. Which of Suzuki's arguments or illustrations is most persuasive? Why?
3. Why does Suzuki stress the biological similarities between people and chimpanzees? What argumentative end is served by the analogy?

Writing Assignments

1. Tell the story of a moment when you realized the difference between right and wrong.
2. Research a pharmaceutical product that you use. The product might be a medicine or a cosmetic. What kinds of tests were used to assure the public that the product was safe for human use?
3. Do you believe that it is morally right or practically necessary to use animals to test medicines for humans? Is it necessary for all medicines or only for those that treat more serious diseases such as AIDS? Write an essay that presents your point of view on animal testing.

Our Animal Rites

Anna Quindlen

Anna Quindlen (1953–) grew up in Philadelphia and graduated from Barnard College. She first worked as a journalist for The New York Post *and* The New York Times, *where she became a personal opinion columnist. Her writing for the* Times' *"Hers" column covers many topics such as motherhood, family relations, and marriage. The best of her columns have been collected in* Living Out Loud *(1988),* Thinking Out Loud *(1993), and* Loud and Clear *(2004). She won the Pulitzer Prize for Commentary in 1992. Her work in fiction includes the novels* Object Lessons *(1991),* One True Thing *(1994),* Black and Blue *(1998), and* Blessings *(2003). The following essay was written as a column in 1990.*

1   The bear had the adenoidal breathing of an elderly man with a passion for cigars and a tendency toward emphysema. My first thought, when I saw him contemplating me through tiny eyes from a rise just beyond the back porch, was that he looked remarkably bearlike, like a close-up shot from a public television nature program.

I screamed. With heavy tread—pad, pad, pad, harrumph, harrumph—the bear went off into the night, perhaps to search for garbage, cans inexpertly closed and apiaries badly lighted. I sat on the porch, shaking. Everyone asks, "Was he big?" My answer is, "Compared to what?"

What I leave out when I tell the story is my conviction that the bear is still watching. At night I imagine he is staring down from the hillside into the lighted porch, as though he had a mezzanine seat for a performance on which the curtain had already gone up. "A nice female, but not very furry," I imagine him thinking, "I see the cubs have gone to the den for the night."

Sometimes I suspect I think this because the peace and quiet of the country have made me go mad, and if only I could hear a car alarm, an ambulance siren, the sound of a boom box playing "The Power" and its owner arguing with his girlfriend over whether or not he was flirting with Denise at the party, all that would drive the bear clear out of my head.

5   Sometimes I think it is because instead of feeling that the bear is   5
trespassing on my property, in my heart I believe that I am trespassing on his.

That feeling is not apparent to city people, although there is something about the sight of a man cleaning up after a sheepdog with a sheet of newspaper that suggests a kind of horrible atonement. The city is a place built by the people, for the people. There we say people are acting like animals when they do things with guns and bats and knives that your ordinary bear would never dream of doing. There we condescend to our animals, with grooming parlors and cat carriers, using them to salve our loneliness and prepare us for parenthood.

All you who lost interest in the dog after the baby was born, you know who you are.

But out where the darkness has depth, where there are no street lights and the stars leap out of the sky, condescension, a feeling of supremacy, what the animal-rights types call speciesism, is impossible. Oh, hunters try it, and it is pathetic to consider the firepower they require to bring down one fair-sized deer. They get three bear days in the autumn, and afterward there is at least one picture in the paper of a couple of smiling guys in hats surrounding the carcass of an animal that looks, though dead, more dignified than they do.

Each spring, after the denning and the long, cold drowse, we wait to see if the bear that lives on the hill above our house beat the bullets. We discover his triumph through signs: a pile of bear dung on the lawn, impossible to assign to any other animal unless mastodons still roam the earth. A garbage box overturned into the swamp, the cole slaw container licked clean. Symmetrical scratch marks five feet up on a tree.

10   They own this land. Once, long ago, someone put a house on it.   10
That was when we were tentative interlopers, when we put a farm-
house here and a barn there. And then we went nuts, built garden con-
dos with pools and office complexes with parking garages and
developments with names that always included the words Park, Acres,
or Hills. You can't stop progress, especially if it's traveling 65 miles an
hour. You notice that more this time of year, when the possums stiffen
by the side of the road.

Sometimes the animals fight back. I was tickled by the people
who bought a house with a pond and paid a good bit of money for a
little dock from which to swim. It did not take long for them to discover that the snapping turtles were opposed to the addition to their
ecosystem of humans wearing sunscreen. An exterminator was sent
for. The pond was dredged. A guest got bit. The turtles won.

I've read that deer use the same trails all their lives. Someone
comes along and puts a neo-Colonial house in the middle of their deer
paths, and the deer will use the paths anyway, with a few detours. If
you watch, you can see that it is the deer that belong and the house
which does not. The bats, the groundhogs, the weasels, the toads—a
hundred years from now, while our family will likely be scattered, their
descendants might be in this same spot. Somewhere out there the bear
is watching, picking his nits and his teeth, breathing his raggedy bear
breath, and if he could talk, maybe he'd say, "I wonder when they're
going back where they belong."

Questions on Meaning

1. Why does Quindlen seem surprised that the bear "looked re-markably bearlike, like a close-up shot from a public television na-ture program"?
2. Quindlen comments of animals: "They own this land." Is she ar-guing that human beings should go somewhere else (and if so, where?). If not, what is her point?
3. What are the animal "rites" the essay's title points to?

Questions on Rhetorical Strategy and Style

1. In at least a couple of places Quindlen personifies the bear by giv-ing it human-like thoughts. What effect does this have in the essay? Does it add to the strength of her argument?
2. Does Quindlen use the techniques of persuasion to attempt to convince the reader? Explain how the essay develops its thesis.

Writing Assignments

1. Quindlen is writing about an area where humans have moved into a natural habitat and seem to be displacing the wildlife there. Some people have argued that humans are not essentially differ-ent from some other animal species, which also become dominant over other species and drive them out or prey upon them. Is it "natural" or "unnatural" for humans to become a dominant species in an area? Does the presence of people automatically mean animals must be displaced, or is some sort of ecological har-mony possible? Write an essay in which you explore the relation-ship between people and wildlife.
2. Looking at yourself from the point of view of an animal can be amusing if not instructive. Write a brief description of yourself going about your daily activities—as you might be seen by a pet such as a dog or cat.

Am I Blue?

Alice Walker

*Alice Walker (1944–) was born in Georgia to sharecrop-
per parents. She attended Spelman College and Sarah
Lawrence College and was active in the civil right movement of the 1960s. Publishing her first novel,* The Third
Life of Garge Copeland, *at the age of 26, she has been a
prolific writer since. In all, she has published five novels,
two short story collections, two collections of essays, and
several books of poems. Her novel* The Color Purple
*(1982) is perhaps her best known, having won the Ameri-
can Book Award, the Pulitzer Prize, and the Candace
Award of the National Coalition of 100 Black Women.
The novel was also made into a prize-wining film by
director Steven Spielberg. Walker's topics run the gamut of
human experience and include some harsh realities such as
incest and racial violence as well as relationships within
familes an society. In the following essay, Walker observes
the behavior of a horse on her neighbor's property, rumi-
nating on how people's treatment of animals often reflects
their treatment of other, less privileged people.*

"Ain't these tears in these eyes tellin' you?"*

1   For about three years my companion and I rented a small house in   1
the country that stood on the edge of a large meadow that
appeared to run from the end of our deck straight into the
mountains. The mountains, however, were quite far away, and between

---

Reprinted from *Living by the Word: Selected Writings 1973–1987*, by permission of
Houghton Mifflin Harcourt Publishing Company. Copyright © 1986 by Alice Walker
and the Wendy Weil Agency.

us and them there was, in fact, a town. It was one of the many pleasant aspects of the house that you never really were aware of this.

It was a house of many windows, low, wide, nearly floor to ceiling in the living room, which faced the meadow, and it was from one of these that I first saw our closest neighbor, a large white horse, cropping grass, flipping its mane, and ambling about—not over the entire meadow, which stretched well out of sight of the house, but over the five or so fenced-in acres that were next to the twenty-odd that we had rented. I soon learned that the horse, whose name was Blue, belonged to a man who lived in another town, but was boarded by our neighbors next door. Occasionally, one of the children; usually a stocky teen-ager, but sometimes a much younger girl or boy, could be seen riding Blue. They would appear in the meadow, climb up on his back, ride furiously for ten or fifteen minutes, then get off, slap Blue on the flanks, and not be seen again for a month or more.

There were many apple trees in our yard, and one by the fence that Blue could almost reach. We were soon in the habit of feeding him apples, which he relished, especially because by the middle of summer the meadow grasses—so green and succulent since January—had dried out from lack of rain and Blue stumbled about munching the dried stalks half-heartedly. Sometimes he would stand very still just by the apple tree, and when one of us came out he would whinny, snort loudly, or stamp the ground. This meant, of course: I want an apple.

It was quite wonderful to pick a few apples, or collect those that had fallen to the ground overnight, and patiently hold them, one by one, up to his large, toothy mouth. I remained as thrilled as a child by his flexible dark lips, huge, cubelike teeth that crunched the apples core and all, with such finality, and his high, broad-breasted *enormity*; beside which, I felt small indeed. When I was a child, I used to ride horses, and was especially friendly with one named Nan until the day I was riding and my brother deliberately spooked her and I was thrown, head first, against the trunk of a tree. When I came to, I was in bed and my mother was bending worriedly over me; we silently agreed that perhaps horseback riding was not the safest sport for me. Since then I have walked, and prefer walking to horseback riding—but I had forgotten the depth of feeling one could see in horses' eyes.

I was therefore unprepared for the expression in Blue's. Blue was lonely. Blue was horribly lonely and bored. I was not shocked that this should be the case; five acres to tramp by yourself, endlessly, even in the most beautiful of meadows—and his was—cannot provide many interesting events, and once rainy season turned to dry that was about it. No, I was shocked that I had forgotten that human animals and nonhuman animals can communicate quite well; if we are brought up around animals as children we take this for granted. By the time we are adults we no longer remember. However, the animals have not changed. They are in fact *completed* creations (at least they seem to be, so much more than we) who are not likely *to* change; it is their nature to express themselves. What else are they going to express? And they do. And, generally speaking, they are ignored.

After giving Blue the apples, I would wander back to the house, aware that he was observing me. Were more apples not forthcoming then? Was that to be his sole entertainment for the day? My partner's small son had decided he wanted to learn how to piece a quilt; we worked in silence on our respective squares as I thought . . .

Well, about slavery: about white children, who were raised by black people, who knew their first all-accepting love from black women, and then, when they were twelve or so, were told they must "forget" the deep levels of communication between themselves and "mammy" that they knew. Later they would be able to relate quite calmly, "My old mammy was sold to another good family." "My old mammy was—— ——." Fill in the blank. Many more years later a white woman would say: "I can't understand these Negroes, these blacks. What do they want? They're so different from us."

And about the Indians, considered to be "like animals" by the "settlers" (a very benign euphemism for what they actually were), who did not understand their description as a compliment.

And about the thousands of American men who marry Japanese, Korean, Filipina, and other non-English-speaking women and of how happy they report they are, "*blissfully*," until their brides learn to speak English, at which point the marriages tend to fall apart. What then did the men see, when they looked into the eyes of the women they married, before they could speak English? Apparently only their own reflections.

I thought of society's impatience with the young. "Why are they playing the music so loud?" Perhaps the children have listened to much of the music of oppressed people their parents danced to before they were born, with its passionate but soft cries for acceptance and love, and they have wondered why their parents failed to hear.

I do not know how long Blue had inhabited his five beautiful, boring acres before we moved into our house; a year after we had arrived—and had also traveled to other valleys, other cities, other worlds—he was still there.

But then, in our second year at the house, something happened in Blue's life. One morning, looking out the window at the fog that lay like a ribbon over the meadow, I saw another horse, a brown one, at the other end of Blue's field. Blue appeared to be afraid of it, and for several days made no attempt to go near. We went away for a week. When we returned, Blue had decided to make friends and the two horses ambled or galloped along together, and Blue did not come nearly as often to the fence underneath the apple tree.

When he did, bringing his new friend with him, there was a different look in his eyes. A look of independence, of self-possession, of inalienable *horse*ness. His friend eventually became pregnant. For months and months there was, it seemed to me, a mutual feeling between me and the horses of justice, of peace. I fed apples to them both. The look in Blue's eyes was one of, unabashed "this is *it*ness."

It did not, however, last forever. One day, after a visit to the city, I went out to give Blue some apples. He stood waiting, or so I thought, though not beneath the tree. When I shook the tree and jumped back from the shower of apples, he made no move. I carried some over to him. He managed to half-crunch one. The rest he let fall to the ground. I dreaded looking into his eyes—because I had of course noticed that Brown, his partner, had gone—but I did look. If I had been born into slavery, and my partner had been sold or killed, my eyes would have looked like that. The children next door explained that Blue's partner had been "put with him" (the same expression that old people used, I had noticed, when speaking of an ancestor during slavery who had been impregnated by her owner) so that they could mate and she conceive. Since that was accomplished, she had been taken back by her owner, who lived somewhere else.

15 Will she be back? I asked. 15

They didn't know.

Blue was like a crazed person. Blue *was*, to me, a crazed person. He galloped furiously, as if he were being ridden, around and around his five beautiful acres. He whinnied until he couldn't. He tore at the ground with his hooves. He butted himself against his single shade tree. He looked always and always toward the road down which his partner had gone. And then, occasionally, when he came up for apples, or I took apples to him, he looked at me. It was a look so piercing, so full of grief, a look so *human*, I almost laughed (I felt too sad to cry) to think there are people who do not know that animals suffer. People like me who have forgotten, and daily forget, all that animals try to tell us. "Everything you do to us will happen to you; we are your teachers, as you are ours. We are one lesson" is essentially it, I think. There are those who never once have even considered animals' rights: those who have been taught that animals actually want to be used and abused by us, as small children "love" to be frightened, or women "love" to be mutilated and raped. . . . They are the great-grandchildren of those who honestly thought, because someone taught them this: "Women can't think," and "niggers can't faint." But most disturbing of all, in Blue's large brown eyes was a new look, more painful than the look of despair: the look of disgust with human beings, with life; the look of hatred. And it was odd what the look of hatred did. It gave him, for the first time, the look of a beast. And what that meant was that he had put up a barrier within to protect himself from further violence; all the apples in the world wouldn't change that fact.

And so Blue remained, a beautiful part of our landscape, very peaceful to look at from the window, white against the grass. Once a friend came to visit and said, looking out on the soothing view: "And it *would* have to be a *white*, horse; the very image of freedom." And I thought, yes, the animals are forced to become for us merely "images" of what they once so beautifully expressed. And we are used to drinking milk from containers showing "contented" cows, whose real lives we want to hear nothing about, eating eggs and drumsticks from "happy" hens, and munching hamburgers advertised by bulls of integrity who seem to command their fate.

As we talked of freedom and justice one day for all, we sat down to steaks. I am eating misery, I thought, as I took the first bite. And spit it out.

Questions on Meaning

1. Why does Walker contend that children have a clearer sense of their connection with animals than adults do? What causes adults to lose that connection?

2. How does Walker interpret the transformation in Blue once Brown has gone? Who is to blame for this transformation?

3. What does Walker mean when she says "I am eating misery"? How does this statement make you feel about humans eating meat?

Questions on Rhetorical Strategy and Style

1. In this essay Walker makes several comparisons between animals and humans, some explicit and some implicit. List these points of comparison and explain their significance in the essay.

2. To what extent does Walker's argument rely on appeals to reason? To emotion? How persuasive do you find her argument? Explain your response.

3. How would you describe Walker's tone in this essay? What features of the essay (i.e., word choice, level of formality, sentence structure) contribute to the tone?

Writing Assignments

1. In a brief essay, respond to Walker's claims about the connection between animals and humans, about animals' feelings, and about animals' rights.

2. Using the parts of Walker's essay that describe Blue, write an essay describing an animal that you have known, focusing not only on the animal's appearance and behavior, but on its personality as well.

3. One of the most prominent animal rights groups in the United States is People for the Ethical Treatment of Animals, or PETA. Consult the organization's website (www.peta.org) and read accounts of its activities in several newspapers and magazines. Then write a profile of the organization, focusing on its core beliefs, its mission, and its goals.

Chimps May Put Their Own Spin on Culture

Bruce Bower

Bruce Bower (1953 –) was born in Los Angeles, Calif. He received his B.A. in psychology from University of California, Berkeley (1975), an M.A. in psychology from Pepperdine University (1976), and an M.A. in journalism from the University of Missouri (1980). He served as a staff writer at Psychiatric News, *a bimonthly publication of the American Psychiatric Association from 1981 to 1983 and has been Behavioral Sciences Editor at* Science News *since 1984. This* Science News *essay provides an important view of animal abilities to develop their own cultures. The essay demonstrates Bower's ability to give life to scientific research and to provide accessible science information for the non-specialist reader.*

1   Chimpanzees don't read or watch television, have no interest in sending their kids to school, and show no inclination for religious worship. Still, a range of evidence suggests that these group-living primates devise their own cultural traditions, according to a new synthesis of field and laboratory studies.

The analysis, published in the December *Current Anthropology*, clashes with the traditional view that attributes culture—a tricky concept to define and study—to humans alone. A minority of investigators has long promoted the idea that chimps and other nonhuman primates, and even whales (SN: 11/28/98, p. 342), invent useful new behaviors and pass them on to kin and fellow group members, a sign of basic cultural capacities.

"A comparison of chimpanzee and human cultures shows many deep similarities, suggesting that they share evolutionary roots," contend Christophe Boesch and Michael Tomasello, both anthropologists at the Max Planck Institute for Evolutionary Anthropology in Leipzig, Germany.

Unlike chimps, however, people pass on knowledge by talking to one another and often assume that others' behaviors are motivated by intentions. These social skills allow humans to modify cultural innovations more quickly and in more varied ways than chimps do, as well as to spread advances over large areas, Boesch and Tomasello hold.

5   The two researchers note that up to now they have been "somewhat at odds" over the question of chimp culture. Boesch had asserted that chimp populations pass along cultural traditions of tool use and communication signals; Tomasello had countered that individual chimps living together may independently invent the same useful behavior, such as using a rock to crack nuts.   5

Current evidence on the daily practices of wild chimps contains many gaps, but it allows for a tentative consensus, the researchers say. They reviewed extensive published material on tool use and other behaviors among African chimp populations in four wildlife areas: Bossou, Gombe, Mahale, and Taï.

Boesch and Tomasello assume that culture involves a set of social learning mechanisms that are used to transmit knowledge to particular individuals. Both chimps and humans exhibit socially learned patterns of activities that last from one generation to the next, they say.

Social influences promote population-specific styles of the same chimp behaviors, the scientists argue. For instance, Taï chimps eat ants by holding a stick with one hand and dipping it among soldier ants guarding their nest entrance. As ants climb the stick, the apes withdraw the tool; with a hand twist, they sweep off insects with their lips.

Gombe chimps also use one hand to place a stick among the same species of soldier ants. But after withdrawing an ant laden probe, they sweep it through the closed fingers of the free hand and then shove the mass of insects into their mouths. Combined with the use of a longer stick, this procedure more efficiently gathers ants than the one observed at Taï, Boesch and Tomasello say.

10   "Ant dipping" and other cultural acts arise through emulation, in   10 which an individual observes a behavior and learns how to use it to

achieve specific goals, they assert. It's less clear whether chimps ever understand the intended results of another's behavior.

Boesch also reports examples of teaching among Taï chimps. Some mothers leave nuts and stone "hammers" in position near anvils for their infants to use. One mother demonstrated a slowed-down version of nut cracking for her child, and another mother modified her son's positioning of a nut for cracking.

The debate continues. Psychologist Bennett G. Galef Jr. of Mc-Master University in Hamilton, Ontario, remains unconvinced that chimps teach or accumulate cultural knowledge. But anthropologist William C. McGrew of Miami University in Oxford, Ohio, says that field studies beyond those in the new report demonstrate cultural capacities of not only chimps but macaque monkeys, too.

Questions on Meaning

1. The essay notes that at one point the two researchers disagreed with one another about chimp tool use. What was the disagreement, and how was it solved?
2. What is the difference between the ant catching behaviors of the two groups observed, and how is this difference interpreted?
3. How do chimps teach their young?

Questions on Rhetorical Strategy and Style

1. The thesis of the essay is that culture is no longer exclusively a human quality. How does the structure of the essay support this thesis?
2. Which examples prove that chimps pass on cultural knowledge just as humans do?

Writing Assignments

1. Define ways in which humans pass on cultural knowledge. Write a paper illustrating one of the methods (i.e., ways of teaching the young, and ways of imitating one another).
2. Investigate two different methods of doing work in American culture, for example, plowing a field with horses or with a tractor. Compare the methods and discuss pros and cons of each.
3. Do further reading about primate research. Write a paper about recent discoveries in the field, arguing for or against primate culture.